# HIDEOUS CAMBRIDGE

## A city mutilated

# HIDEOUS CAMBRIDGE

## A city mutilated

David Jones

Photographs by Ellis Hall

Thirteen Eighty One

First published 2013 by Thirteen Eighty One LLP

Thirteen Eighty One LLP

website: www.thirteeneightyone.com
facebook: thirteeneightyone
email: info@thirteeneightyone.com

ISBN 978-0-9926073-0-2

Set in MS Georgia 10 pt

Printed by Cambridge Print Solutions
website: www.cambridgeprintsolutions.co.uk
email: info@cambridgeprintsolutions.co.uk
tel: 01223 242000

# Contents

# Preface

This work is neither a guide nor a gazetteer, but simply one individual's response to the ugly face of Cambridge. As a consequence, some places and buildings receive more mention in its pages than others, and many that might be expected to feature in a publication about the city receive none at all. Its primary focus is on the outward appearance of buildings and the impression they make on the man in the street, and while it gives some historical context and occasionally refers to writers on architecture, it is a polemic rather than an academic study.

During its preparation, the pace of change in Cambridge became so rapid as to require revision of the text on almost a weekly basis, and while this final version is now fixed in time, reflecting the situation in August 2013, change continues remorselessly. It is therefore likely that some of the observations made here have already been overtaken by events.

The majority of the photographs are by Ellis Hall. His offer to take them was gladly accepted, and our frequent discussions during the project have been most helpful. About twenty are my own, each identified by my initials, and several old photos from the Cambridgeshire Collection are similarly initialled. For permission to use the latter, I am very grateful to Chris Jakes, whose unfailing and courteous assistance must figure in so many authors' acknowledgements.

I am also grateful to the following people who read through the entire text and made extremely valuable observations, suggestions and corrections. In alphabetical order, they are: Clare Allen, Allan Brigham, Jeff Bushrod, Angela Donnelly, Melissa Good, Bryony Hall, Lilian Hall, John and Betsy McNeill, Bridget Somekh and Nick Toop.

Finally, I must single out Lilian Hall for particular praise. She spent many hours carefully scrutinising the drafts, not only spotting typing blunders of the smallest and most elusive kind, but also drawing attention to passages too cryptic or opaque to pass muster. This book would have been much poorer without her admirable work.

# Introduction: the view from the street

If, on entering Trinity Great Court, you saw a skip of rubbish surmounted by a cracked lavatory bowl in place of the centrepiece fountain, what would your reaction be? Similar to mine, no doubt, when one afternoon I was cycling past the Victorian houses of Glisson Road and saw a Brutalist office block barging across the view in front of me: 'My God, how hideous!' That was the moment when the idea for this book came into being. Why not produce an alternative guide to Cambridge, one that paints a more realistic picture than the clichéd postcards and guide books, with their views of King's Chapel, college gardens and punts on the river? And so in 2010 I began to investigate the lesser known and less beautiful parts of the city; those that do not feature in Tourist Board brochures and on travel agents' websites.

But my objective soon began to change. I had been aware for some time that the future of Cambridge could involve considerable growth, but so far this had appeared to remain a matter of discussion and debate. Then, as my work progressed, new and awful buildings began to go up with increasing frequency. Large redevelopment projects were announced, and 'eco-villages' were proposed every other week, until the speed of change and the damage to the city grew more and more reckless. It became increasingly apparent that Cambridge was on the brink of possibly the biggest change to its size and fabric since the 19th-century Enclosure Acts enabled new building to take place beyond the old centre. It seemed that all the caution which for so long had characterised Cambridge planning was being abruptly thrown aside, and pouring in through the wide-open gates were the developers, eager to make a killing. The implications of this are alarming: economic and population growth, university and civic ambitions, and pressure from central government are creating the prospect of the city swelling into a conurbation almost the size of Birmingham. Cambridge as we know it is in danger of being utterly ruined.

The book thus changed in character and purpose. Far from writing a guide, I found myself writing a polemic. I began to see that the ugliness around me lay not only in ill-designed or inappropriately placed buildings, but also in the motives that sometimes lay behind their construction, and in their disturbing social consequences. The development proposals also raised the question of how large Cambridge should be, and at what point expansion would destroy much of what we value about our city, in particular its comfortable size with open country no more than a short bike ride away, its many green open spaces, the human scale of its buildings and the absence of tower blocks.

Not everyone will agree with the views given in this book: any judgement about the aesthetic merits of a building, for example, will inevitably contain subjective elements. But in the light of the considerable hostility I have heard expressed towards many recent buildings and proposals for the future, it appears that I am not alone in my opinions. It therefore seems to me essential that something be said – something more substantial and sustained than an irate letter to the local press – about the direction in which Cambridge is apparently heading; disgracefully bad developments should not be allowed to happen without emphatic protest, if only as a record for posterity.

It will be clear from this study that I am not an architect, a planner or a developer. I have no vested interests of that kind. I write merely as one who has lived in Cambridge for four decades. I hope I speak for others who 'just live here' and have to put up with the abominations that now almost daily seem to be announced or constructed. And while I am not professionally involved in designing buildings and urban landscapes, I have lived in and read about them enough to have a reasonably informed opinion on the quality of my surroundings. You don't have to be an 'expert' to see that the Hills Road bridge area, for example, is a disaster, built recently as if nothing had been learnt from past mistakes. It suggests that those 'experts' of planning and design either inhabit a perversely different world from the rest of us, or simply do not care about the visual atrocities they are committing; or perhaps that other considerations, such as money or government housing targets, are paramount.

The extent to which Cambridge will grow is not yet clear. When this book was almost complete, many of the fears expressed in it were confirmed by the council's 2012 draft Local Plan for Cambridge. This did contain a number of encouraging proposals, though some gave the distinct impression that the authors had only just woken up. The policy on protecting the city's skyline, for example, has come too late to prevent the damage already done in just the past six years. Nevertheless, while it may prove impossible to check the city's expansion, it ought to be possible to demand better standards of design, not only in materials and colour, but most importantly in scale and profile, for only in this way can we ensure that the unique character of Cambridge is respected. In recent years such respect has been disastrously lacking. Showing respect does not necessarily mean harmonising, copying or creating a pastiche. Good contemporary design can yet be sympathetic to earlier work, as in the case of the Jerwood Library at Trinity Hall. Too many contemporary buildings in Cambridge, however, refer to nothing on earth.

This book does not aim to be a comprehensive gazetteer but is very much a selection, and while its main focus is on ugly buildings, it does examine instructive examples of good new architecture and older buildings of merit. After considering first impressions along the approaches by road and rail, it looks at the centre and then works outwards to the early suburbs which have been partly redeveloped (New Town, Barnwell, Sturton Town and Romsey Town), the outer suburbs which are now also threatened by damaging change, the riverside, and the city's fringes. Two chapters then take particular themes before the book concludes with three chapters on signs of things to come.

I might add that I probably refer to things Danish often enough for it to be noticeable. Denmark is a country I know well, and I have been impressed by the quality of its buildings and street furniture. The Danes have made their mistakes too, but in general they seem to give more care to the details of the built environment, and their example is worth noting. There is also more than one uncomplimentary remark about Birmingham, so I should make it clear that I was born there and know what I am talking about. The Birmingham suburb of Bournville was my home for the first eighteen years of my life, and it too features by way of illustration. The blight of motor traffic is a more conspicuous thread running through this book, for which, as one of the many cyclists in Cambridge, I make no apology. It even has a chapter to itself.

The Royal Fine Art Commission, in its report for 1955-6, had this to say on the topic of buildings and their design; 'the rights of the man in the street deserve the same consideration as those of the man in the office, or his landlord.' This book is the voice of one such man in the street.

# 1

# Cambridge: the setting

For most of its existence Cambridge has been small. It began as a Roman camp on Castle Hill, and the Saxon settlement that followed occupied the area around Market Hill. The subsequent medieval town was confined almost entirely to the area bounded by the river and the King's Ditch, which ran in an arc from Mill Lane to Jesus Green. Outside lay huge open fields and commons, farmed collectively according to medieval custom. At the start of the 19th century the town was little bigger in area than it had been during the middle ages.

The Enclosure Acts of 1802 and 1807 allowed Cambridge to grow beyond its medieval boundaries. The West and East Fields were reorganised, and land-owners had their scattered strips of land grouped into more convenient parcels which they were free to farm, sell, or build on. The Acts were essentially designed to improve agriculture, but they also made possible the physical growth of the town when other causes led the population to rise, and they constituted the most significant change in the town's history until recent times.

Enclosures often included the common land. Fortunately, the Cambridge commons flooded too often and in consequence were left alone. The town therefore retained an exceptional inner green ring running from Coe Fen through the Backs to Jesus Green and Midsummer Common, as well as outer green spaces at Stourbridge and Coldham's Commons to the east and Grantchester Meadows to the south. This was later enhanced by the donation of Parker's Piece.

Elsewhere, building development eventually took place. It was gradual at first and also piecemeal, occurring as individual landowners decided to sell. The earliest developments followed existing roads, more or less as ribbon development. Thus houses appeared along Trumpington Road and Regent Street, Newmarket Road and East Road. Infilling followed, to create the suburb of Barnwell to the east and New Town to the south of Downing College.

The coming of the railway in 1845 led to further expansion to the south-east. After 1850 Sturton Town was built on either side of Mill Road up to the railway line, and then, from the 1880s, Romsey Town grew up beyond it. Building also began to spread off Hills Road beyond Cherry Hinton Road, while north of the river, Huntingdon Road and Chesterton began to see new housing.

To the west there was very little development. Mercifully, most of the land belonged to the colleges and they were not seduced by short-term speculation and quick profits. College gardens and playing fields were laid out, but building only began in earnest after 1882, when college Fellows were allowed to marry and family houses began to be provided for them. The expansion of education also brought new building to the west in the last quarter of the 19th century; Newnham College, Selwyn College, Ridley Hall and King's College Choir School were all built at this time. In contrast to the density of development to the east and southeast, west Cambridge remained spacious.

The growth of the town during the 19th century and the increased scope of local government responsibility led to the construction of many public buildings, both in the centre and in the new suburbs. Churches, schools, libraries, hospitals, police and fire stations, workhouses and a prison were all required. The expansion of the university brought new colleges, a museums site and laboratories. Consequently the building trades prospered and brick works and cement quarries sprang up, mostly to the north and south of Coldham's Common. However, Cambridge was spared any large-scale industrial development and there was no Cowley car plant such as spoiled Oxford.

The 20th century saw continued expansion. The town boundary was frequently revised until it absorbed Chesterton, Newnham, Trumpington and Cherry Hinton. Villages just outside – Girton, Histon, Impington, Milton, Fen Ditton, Teversham, Fulbourn, Grantchester – now looked particularly vulnerable, only just retaining their independence. Council building as well as private development led to more infilling between the radial roads. An inter-war suburbia sprang up and was enlarged post-war; King's Hedges, Arbury, Ditton Fields, Coleridge, Queen Edith's and Chesterton all grew, while, to the west, smaller and more exclusive areas were developed off Madingley and Trumpington Roads. On the eastern side of the city, development was checked by the green expanses of Coldham's Common and Marshall's airfield which, to this day, along with the lakes on the former site of the Norman cement works, provide a welcome absence of built-up land and its inevitable concomitant, motor traffic.

But as early as 1948 there was sufficient pressure from new development to cause alarm at the direction in which Cambridge was moving. As a result

*The growth of Cambridge*

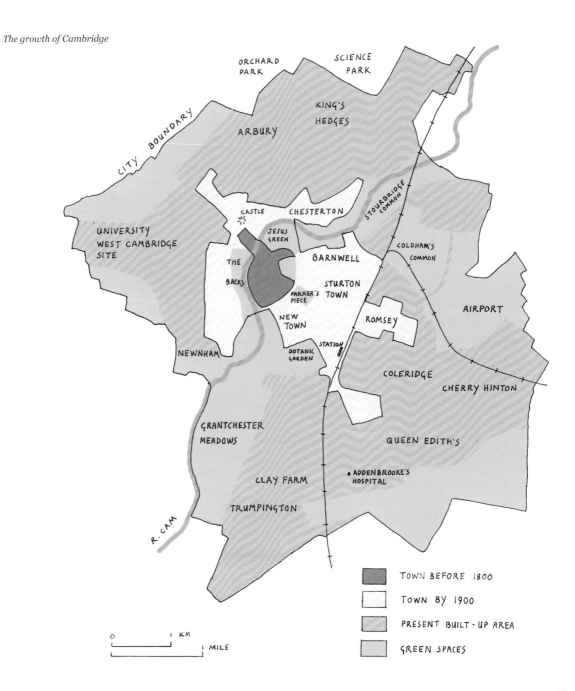

ORCHARD PARK

SCIENCE PARK

KING'S HEDGES

ARBURY

CITY BOUNDARY

CASTLE

CHESTERTON

STOURBRIDGE COMMON

JESUS GREEN

UNIVERSITY WEST CAMBRIDGE SITE

THE BACKS

BARNWELL

COLDHAM'S COMMON

PARKER'S PIECE

STURTON TOWN

NEW TOWN

ROMSEY

AIRPORT

NEWNHAM

BOTANIC GARDEN

STATION

COLERIDGE

CHERRY HINTON

GRANTCHESTER MEADOWS

QUEEN EDITH'S

CLAY FARM

• ADDENBROOKE'S HOSPITAL

TRUMPINGTON

R. CAM

0        1 KM

1 MILE

TOWN BEFORE 1800

TOWN BY 1900

PRESENT BUILT-UP AREA

GREEN SPACES

Cambridgeshire County Council commissioned William Holford, Professor of Town Planning at the University of London, to draw up proposals for a development plan. He was assisted by H. Myles Wright, a colleague in the Ministry of Town and Country Planning, and 'Cambridge Planning Proposals', more usually known as the Holford Report, came out in 1950. It identified rapid growth and pressure of traffic as the two chief problems and concluded that continued rapid growth was undesirable. A population of 125,000 was considered to be the proper limit. 'One cannot make a good expanding plan for Cambridge', said the authors; a large increase in size would destroy the incomparable advantages and amenities that Cambridge enjoyed, bringing nothing valuable in return.

The report also urged the preservation of the Green Belt that separated Girton, Fen Ditton and Grantchester from the city. Any growth, it stated, should retain a compact city. It recommended that building heights should normally remain low, especially in and near the city centre. Fortunately, its proposal for a 'Spine Relief Road', which would have cut across Christ's Pieces, was not adopted. There were many other interesting points of detail, and the report still makes relevant reading today. Its broad proposals were followed and Cambridge did not grow into the large, sprawling city it might have become. Only recently have Holford's precepts been openly challenged.

Developments since 1950 have kept the matter of growth versus potential damage in the forefront of planners' minds. In 1965 the British Association for the Advancement of Science met in Cambridge. In one of the essays in 'The Cambridge Region', published for the meeting, university lecturer A.A.L. Caesar wrote of future trends. He saw Cambridge becoming both a dormitory of London and an attractive place for firms to move to, a situation all the more likely to occur given the planned electrification of the King's Cross railway line and the construction of the M11. There was the risk that Cambridge might become 'an industrial duplicate of Harlow or Stevenage'. He urged action to control these damaging forces and warned, 'Megalopolis … is upon us'.

His predictions were right. He even foresaw the building of Stansted Airport and its consequences. London commuting and migration into the area have increased the pressures on Cambridge. So too has the unanticipated 'Cambridge Phenomenon' of the 1980s. The growth of the Science Park south of Milton has brought specialised high-tech employment and the

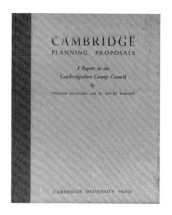

*The Holford Report, published in 1950, urged restraint on growth in Cambridge and advised an upper limit of 125,000 inhabitants.*

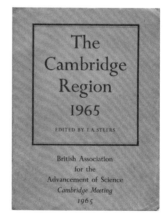

*In 1965 the British Association for the Advancement of Science debated the future of Cambridge and accurately predicted many of today's damaging trends.*

establishment of similar businesses in and around Cambridge. Fortunately they do not individually require huge work forces or vast acres of land, but the cumulative effect is growing. Addenbrooke's Hospital, on the other hand, does have a large work force – over 8,000 staff at the last count – and the policy of creating a 'super hospital' and biomedical research centre is resulting in what looks like a small town in itself. The expansion of higher education has also meant more building, and the rise of tourism has added new pressures, along with more hotels. 'Leisure' requires more facilities than formerly, whether they be gyms or clubs or cinemas. Even shopping has become a 'leisure activity', drawing thousands into Cambridge and resulting in ever more grandiose shopping malls.

The Holford policy of limiting growth in the city has led to the expansion of existing villages and the building of new ones lying just beyond the Green Belt (established in 1955). But instead of providing new centres of employment, the communities of Bar Hill and Cambourne have become dormitories for workers who cannot afford to live in the city. The consequences for traffic we know only too well. Northstowe, a projected development of 9,500 homes, will be no different. Plans for similar settlements have been made and, if built, all of these 'eco-villages' will orbit Cambridge and regard it as their place for work, shopping and leisure.

That is bad enough. But the situation has been made worse in the past decade by the abandonment of the limits on growth. There are pressures to fill up whatever space is left in the city and to relax the Green Belt, allowing the fringes to spread towards the satellite settlements. This is precisely the kind of outward creep that the Belt was designed to prevent, for once it begins it is hard to stop. The city boundary could easily be redrawn as it has been in the past (indeed the current Local Plan implies this intention), and in no time Cambridge could grow to the size of Birmingham.

If this seems an exaggeration, take a map, put a compass point in the centre of Birmingham and draw a circle with a radius of five miles. Then do the same for Cambridge. The first circle will cover almost all of Birmingham. The second, centred on Cambridge, will take in villages that could easily be engulfed: Hauxton, Shelford and Stapleford to the south, Fulbourn to the east, Waterbeach, Histon, Girton, Oakington to the north. The settlements at Bar Hill, Cambourne and Hardwick have already been developed, Northstowe is to come and developers are casting avaricious eyes on

OSCOTT

ERDINGTON

HANDSWORTH     ASTON

SHARD END

● CITY
  CENTRE

YARDLEY

EDGBASTON

SELLY OAK

HALL
GREEN

BOURNVILLE

NORTHFIELD     KINGS
               NORTON

RUBERY                    DJJ 2012

*This and facing page: Birmingham and Cambridge compared up to a radius of five miles.*

Hinxton, Waterbeach, Six Mile Bottom and the area from Marshall's airfield towards Teversham and Fulbourn. While pockets of open land would no doubt remain, it is not fanciful to suppose that a new, greater Cambridge could emerge to equal the size of Britain's 'Second City'. This is already happening by increments and happening, moreover, without popular consent. People choose to live here precisely because it is not Birmingham, yet the present tendency is to destroy the advantages and amenities of a small town. That destruction would be irreversible.

COTTENHAM

LONGSTANTON

WESTWICK
LANDBEACH
WATERBEACH

OAKINGTON
HISTON
IMPINGTON
MILTON
HORNINGSEA

BAR HILL

GIRTON

DRY DRAYTON

MADINGLEY
STOW-
CUM-
QUY
FEN DITTON

HARDWICK
COTON
CITY
CENTRE
TEVERSHAM

FULBOURN

COMBERTON
GRANTCHESTER
BARTON
TRUMPINGTON

WANDLEBURY

HASLINGFIELD
HAUXTON
ST.
LT. SHELFORD
STAPLEFORD

HARSTON

DJJ 2012

The threat increased in 2012, with a government proposal to revise the Town and Country Act (1947) to give a presumption in favour of 'sustainable development', those meaningless words uttered to defend unwanted eyesores. ('You don't want a tower block next to the Botanic Garden?! But it's *sustainable*!') The effect will be to weaken local control. If a developer's scheme is refused permission, he may appeal to the Planning Inspector with every confidence that the verdict will be in his favour. Additionally, the recognition that 'ordinary' countryside has value is likely to be removed from the Act. If green fields and open space are not of exceptional beauty, they will be deemed to have no merit at all, save as building sites. It remains to be seen how far the National Trust and other pressure groups will be able to modify this builders' charter.

Over a period of almost a thousand years Cambridge has acquired some extraordinarily fine buildings. It has also acquired some exceptionally nasty ones. Many of the latter have arrived in relatively recent times as a consequence of hasty growth, speculation, industrial building techniques and new materials. Erosion of distinctively local qualities has also occurred because of 'globalisation' and the internationalisation of building styles. As long ago as 1934, French novelist André Gide wrote this about Prague, a city venerated by today's tourists for being supposedly 'unspoilt': 'Very strange city; made somewhat ugly by non-indigenous contributions, a sort of American or Sovietic modernism...' ('Journals', 5 August 1934). Plenty of non-indigenous elements have reached Cambridge in recent years to bring its appearance closer to Anytown.

The Cambridge of the Backs is only a small part of the picture. If you were making your first visit and you came by rail, would you know that you were arriving at an ancient university town famed for its buildings? Or would you think you were arriving at Reading? Or Stevenage? For that is the way Cambridge is heading.

# 2

# 'Gateways': the approaches

*This chapter examines the general impressions a first-time visitor might receive on entering Cambridge by any of the main routes into the city, and introduces the themes explored in this book. Without attempting to be a gazetteer, it also directs the reader's attention to particularly striking buildings and features along these approaches.*

## The railway

Railway approaches can be exciting in the glimpses and vistas they afford, such as the spectacular view of Ely Cathedral or the first sight of Oxford's skyline. They can more often be depressing and sordid, marred by the untidy yards, warehouses, workshops, abandoned sidings and terraced houses that inevitably grow up around the station of a large town. Cambridge falls into this second category.

From the north there is a single tantalising glimpse of the pinnacles and towers of the colleges seen as one crosses the river at Stourbridge Common. Then one runs the gauntlet of industrial units, new apartments crammed against the track, and the ugly backsides of Great Eastern Street.

*Nearing Cambridge station from the north, rail visitors encounter the huge LNWR locomotive depot, which sets the perfect tone for their first impressions of the city.*

From the south, after a pleasant countrified scene, the alarming piles of the Addenbrooke's Biomedical Campus loom up, followed by the warrens of new flats likely to be the slums of the future. It appears that one is arriving not at an ancient seat of learning but at the land of the luckless commuter.

First impressions matter, and the railway traveller to Cambridge will so far be unimpressed. Platform signs seem to insinuate that Anglia Ruskin University is the city's pre-eminent educational institution, while the station's congested ticket hall with nowhere to sit or take stock is lamentably unwelcoming. The waiting room is poky, the lavatories inadequate, and the refreshment facilities sparse. There is not even a decent clock, either on the platform or in the ticket hall. The station's amenities are, in fact, too limited for the huge numbers travelling today.

*Marketing spin masquerades as visitor information - is this the right Cambridge? Or has the hapless visitor entered the Twilight Zone?*

But it is on stepping out of the station that one is most shocked. Despite the efforts of Victorian worthies who created a tree-lined avenue to Hills Road, the immediate vicinity has been for years a disastrously untidy mess of miscellaneous decrepit buildings and hoardings, not to mention an enormous bicycle graveyard. Circulation for traffic and pedestrians is chaotically intermingled and dangerous. At regular intervals, hordes of passengers, disgorged from crowded trains, pour out of the station directly into the path of jostling cars, buses and taxis. There are no signs, no obvious direction in which to head. Where is a visitor to go? Which way is the city centre? Where is the university? Where is the Cambridge of the guide books?

*Nearing Cambridge station from the south, rail visitors are treated to views suggesting arrival at a dreary London dormitory town.*

Well, the area is currently being developed to create a suitably impressive 'gateway' to Cambridge. Will this be an improvement? Not necessarily. The original proposals were, unsurprisingly, received with horror and hostility, even by city councillors. Are we afraid of the buildings of our own time? Yes we are, and with good reason. After all, we have had plenty of failures set before us. That buzzword 'gateway' was used to justify the originally planned, massively out-of-scale, glass and concrete blocks whose upper storeys would have been visible for literally miles outside Cambridge, and which showed no respect for the one building of merit in the area – the station itself.

*Cambridge Railway Station, built in 1845, has an elegance and refinement unmatched by its new neighbours.*

One would not claim that the developers were consciously wanting to put up inappropriate buildings; their intention, presumably, was to improve the site and provide something 'worthy' of Cambridge. But there will always be a conflict between doing something architecturally pleasing on the one hand and something that maximises profit on the other, and this inevitably leads to the risk of overdevelopment. What is more, the desire to make an impact can backfire into 'sensation-seeking stunts', as Herman Muthesius called them back in 1904, in his highly perceptive book 'The English House'. The choice of architect for the project exemplified this – a high-profile, prestigious, internationally renowned, cutting-edge practice famous for making big statements in novel ways. The resulting designs were aggressive, edgy and overbearing. Modesty and restraint were to be dwarfed by flashy, metropolitan 'look-at-me' buildings wholly at variance with the *genius loci* of Cambridge.

*Cambridge, ancient university town of outstanding beauty. Is this it?*

The plan for the forecourt, published in June 2013, shows improved traffic circulation but scant green landscaping and a heavy, looming block as depressing as the one that has already gone up in Station Place. The long, dull range of the latter incorporates Foster's Mill as it draws its dreary length away to the left, and a good opportunity to demolish the mill – a building of no architectural merit and meagre historical value – has been lost. Station Road itself is due to be lined with seven- and eight-storey office blocks which will create an unpleasant canyon to greet the visitor. This, then, will be the 'gateway' to Cambridge, but not the Cambridge of the world-famous university with its exceptional architecture. Rather, it will be the Cambridge of shopping malls, office blocks, hotel complexes, rabbit-warren apartments and Anglia Ruskin University.

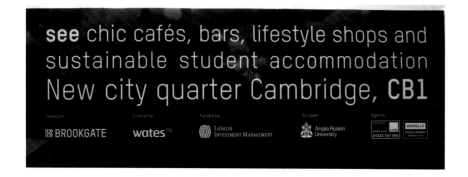

*Chic, shallow and superficial. Is this abject surrender to consumerism a sign of the new Cambridge?*

## The approaches by road

Many medieval towns had real gateways in encircling walls. While they survive in places like Canterbury, Chester and King's Lynn, most have been pulled down to accommodate traffic and are now remembered only in the names of shopping centres and electoral wards – Northgate in Oxford, for example, or Westgate in Ipswich and Newcastle. Cambridge once had the Barnwell and Trumpington gates at the King's Ditch, but these were not of any size, and there were no walls. Gates and walls marked the entry to most towns and they told you that you had arrived. Even as late as the mid-eighteenth century there was still a clear distinction between town and country, as can be seen in the prints made by the Buck brothers. Towns then had a clear spatial identity set in the surrounding landscape. Their important buildings, notably church spires and towers, were clearly visible.

Today, suburban sprawl has blurred the lines. By the early 20th century, outlying houses, bungalows, or petrol stations became the first signs of an approaching town. Now it is more likely to be a ring road, a vast roundabout with signs saying City North, City South, a superstore with associated car park, and a drift of litter along the verges. The town boundary is clearly visible only on a map, and the first inkling you might have of crossing it could be when you see a sign saying 'Welcome to Toytown, home of Noddy', or whatever local connection the council wishes to promote.

### The Hills Road approach

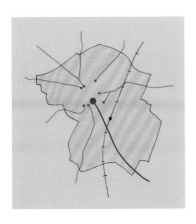

*The Hills Road approach, entering Cambridge from the southeast along the A1307.*

The approach from the southeast, over the Gog Magog Hills, is the most spectacular and the most vulnerable. Passing the Iron Age fort at Wandlebury on the right, one sees the whole of Cambridge spread out in the plain below. This is the view that the Cambridge Preservation Society famously sought to protect in 1936. Its 'Save the Gogs' campaign depicted ribbon development reaching out towards Wandlebury like the tentacles of an octopus (a reference to the polemic by Clough Williams-Ellis, 'England and the Octopus', published in 1928). The Society was able to prevent further despoilation then, but new threats and actual blights have appeared since. The eye is no longer drawn to the pinnacles of King's Chapel or the tower of St John's, or even Ely Cathedral on the dim horizon, but to Addenbrooke's Hospital, the most blatant and glaring eruption on the southern landscape. It squats like a separate settlement around a 260-foot high incinerator chimney that is visible for miles and seems to raise two fingers to the old university town two miles distant.

Alas, there is really nothing to be done about Addenbrooke's. It is a necessary institution and there are good reasons for turning it into a bio-medical campus of regional, national, even global importance. While the newest buildings have some architectural distinction, it is nonetheless a misfortune that health care now requires construction on an industrial scale. It is equally unfortunate that so vast a complex should be sited in open landscape on the visually sensitive south side of Cambridge, the very area the Preservation Society fought to protect from speculative housing almost 80 years ago.

The speculative housing is now under way too. We await the completion of Clay Farm, just west of Addenbrooke's, with trepidation. It has already had its name taken away – no doubt as being too *infra dig* for a housing estate – and replaced with a marketing-inspired, mock-heritage label that might belong to a new cheese and which few will spell correctly. 'Great Kneighton', as we must now call it, will not be a garden suburb, we can be sure of that.

*Addenbrooke's Hospital viewed from Wandlebury. Imagine the landscape without it.*

*The incinerator chimney.*

Modest two-storey houses built to a low density and blended into the landscape are not as lucrative as three-storey town houses or four- to five-storey apartment blocks. And there are government building targets to meet as well. Look on Orchard Park (Chapter 13) and despair.

The first homes to be finished at Great Kneighton/Clay Farm are much as one might have predicted. Sure enough, there are flat-roofed apartment blocks of three to five storeys, and while individual units are smart and of tasteful design, their height and density seem more suited to a highly urban site rather than one on the edge of open country. We shall have to wait until the whole development is complete to see how far tree planting and parkland, which is already underway, will soften the impact of its projected density.

Leaving our vantage point on the Gogs we descend towards leafy suburbia. There is the inevitable petrol station to pass, a car showroom, and a Park and Ride site decently screened by trees but with compulsory floodlighting to brighten up one's evenings. After a solitary farm on our right, houses begin to appear, large, inoffensive and tree shaded, but this pleasant prospect is only a brief interlude, for within a short space of time the sprawling entrance to Addenbrooke's Hospital appears, brutally exposed by the recent felling of trees for almost a hundred yards along a car park boundary. As we pass it and crest the short rise up to the junction with Long Road, we are confronted with a view that runs for three quarters of a mile down a tree-lined suburban road to the most shocking tower block, a structure utterly out of scale and out of harmony with its surroundings. This oppressive eyesore marks the dystopian treeless nightmare that we reach at the railway bridge, an area so appalling it has a chapter to itself. For the moment, we will give it some hasty glances and hurry on.

*An eye-watering jump in scale. Approaching the railway bridge from the south, Victorian survivals give way to The Levels and The Belvedere.*

The Belvedere's metal-clad tower, a
'landmark' feature not to be confused
with a fire escape.

But before we do, let us turn to see the way we have come and what we are leaving behind. The photo at the top of the facing page, taken in May 2005, shows a leafy avenue marred only by the inevitable street furniture and lamp posts taller than the trees. To turn back 180 degrees is to confront a ghastly contrast. It is as if we have been transported to Docklands.

On the left, two-storey buildings give way to a pair of multistorey cliffs, culminating in the Dalek-like tower of The Belvedere, a so-called 'landmark' building. While there is at least a harmony of style and brick colour in these new structures, and while they grow up in stages from their lower Victorian neighbour, their façades are messily punctuated by fashionable 'Juliet' balconies in the sort of grey that resembles the plastic trim on toy guns. They clutter the otherwise clean surfaces and would seem to be without practical purpose other than as a repository for greenery to hide the view; the cacophonous maelstrom of traffic below and its noxious exhalations mock any notion of sitting out for fresh air, or even calling out for Romeo.

*Above: The Marque - a visual catastrophe of staggering proportions - under construction at the junction of Hills Road and Cherry Hinton Road.*

On the right, at the corner of Cherry Hinton Road, stands the tower we saw from a distance – The Marque; outrageous, vile, pretentious and a positive disgrace. This horror is discussed more fully in Chapter 14. On the further side of Cherry Hinton Road is the bizarrely aligned Travelodge hotel with adjacent leisure buildings of stunning mediocrity. Development on both sides of the bridge seems to have been uncoordinated and *ad hoc* – or at least so one hopes, for it would be depressing to think that this disaster were in any way premeditated.

*Below: Neither an academy nor a house, and judging by the artist's impression, no better than the existing buildings in this architectural disaster zone.*

Over the bridge more unpleasantness lies in store. To the left are offices thrown up since the late 1980s in the hope of speculative profits. City House (1990), on the corner of Brooklands Avenue, was refused final approval by city planners for contravening regulations on maximum building height, and remained an unfinished, decaying and unoccupied shell for well over a decade. Only after substantial rebuilding in 2002 were some of its units let. The billboard beside it announces another accomplished horror, the forth-coming Academy House, which displays the kind of architecture the developers, who are based at a stately home in rural Suffolk, think is good enough for the likes of Cambridge. ('May be sub divided into smaller units'.)

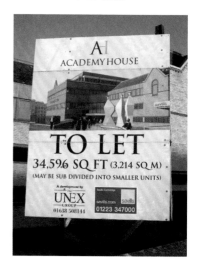

Incidentally, could there be a ban on the use of words like 'academy', 'college' and 'scholars' in association with buildings entirely unrelated to such things? What is wrong with calling a building 'Railway Bridge House' or 'Signal Box View'? Then at least you would know where to look for it.

*A leafy prospect - Hills Road looking south from the junction with Cherry Hinton Road.*

*The view north from virtually the same spot. Not a tree in sight.*

Beyond where Academy House is going to stand, more apartment blocks have gone up on the old Cambridge University Press site in quantities reminiscent of Eastern Europe under Communism. The perpetrators of 'Kaleidoscope' – discussed more fully in Chapter 12 – boast of the unique 'Vision' and 'Lifestyle' built into their garish creation, but not of the fine view it affords of the railway track and the Belvedere ('ideal for train spotters'), not to mention 'Signal Box View' when it comes. Neither do they mention the hours of fun residents will have when attempting to join traffic-choked Brooklands Avenue on a weekday morning.

The north side of the bridge has also seen changes, with the area on the right being opened up by a new road to the railway station, something that was proposed decades ago. The demolition of existing buildings to make way for the road resulted in the ugly flats of The Triangle becoming visible from Hills Road, until they were hidden from view once more by the massive and spectacularly bland 'gateway' blocks of cb1. The mediocrity of the cb1 development is also examined in Chapter 12.

*The Royal Albert Almshouses.*

*Botanic House, vastly out of scale with its neighbours and wholly ignorant of its impact on the immediate surroundings, which include the War Memorial and the University Botanic Garden.*

After all this, it is a pleasure to set eyes on the Royal Albert Almshouses. They are perfectly set in the angle of Hills Road and Brooklands Avenue, are of satisfying human proportions and possess nice attention to detail – in the ridge tiles, the decorative brickwork and the caps of the gateposts. Even the clock still works. City House tried to refer to it with pointed gables and similar brickwork (see p. 216), but it was like an elephant trying to disguise itself as a greyhound. Copying a motif or two is no good; such mimicry is mere lip service to the notion of respecting existing buildings.

Next we come to Station Road, where further atrocities can be expected. If evidence were wanted of today's priorities, we need only point to the removal of the War Memorial out of the way of the traffic. Very good of the

*Human-scale buildings in Hills Road, enhanced by a genuine Cambridge landmark - the Church of Our Lady and the English Martyrs.*

developers to suggest placing it where it can't impede or be seen by the motorists hurrying by, but one might have thought that the whole point of such a memorial was to make people stop and think. Instead, one's attention is drawn to, and shocked by, the out-of-scale and meretricious Botanic House, constructed while this book was being researched. This lamentable building, tightly squeezed in like a fat cuckoo on a tiny nest, presents a ludicrous and unsettling shift of scale, which utterly and disrespectfully dwarfs the War Memorial. (See photo on p. 243.)

Botanic House is considered further in Chapters 10, 12 and 14; that gives an indication of its catastrophic impact.

From Station Road to the city centre we meet 19th-century ribbon developments of shops, churches and large former private houses, mingled with 20th-century offices and modern alterations. Many of the 19th-century buildings must have seemed drab even when new, but their human scale redeems them to the pedestrian who is so frequently assaulted by overweight office blocks. Immediately on our left, past the Botanic Garden, there are several such blocks that alter the scale of the street, good examples of ill-judged Modernism.

*Charter House (below), and the former Three Crowns House (bottom) - 20th-century office blocks both given 21st-century makeovers.*

*Terrington House - slick metropolitan glitz in St Paul's Road.*

Other mediocre modern intrusions line this road, but there is also a remarkable survival that was very nearly destroyed. Cintra House was spared complete demolition on account of its unusual façade, which was preserved while the rooms behind it were rebuilt to modern requirements. This might be seen as a bit of fakery, but the façade was well worth keeping. A modern block would not have matched its charm. The details have been admirably maintained, and the Open University has had the sense to use a simple and dignified logo to indicate its occupancy of the building.

On the other side of the road stands Terrington House. This office block demonstrates the advantages of modern steel frame and concrete construction. The shell can be entirely re-clad, and a new image presented, without the expense of complete demolition and rebuilding. Whether the glitzy new exterior is desirable in this location is debatable. It is all right, no doubt, if you want Cambridge to look 'metropolitan' and 'cutting edge' – and anonymously like any other pushy city. Since the 1960s, new buildings replacing demolitions have suffered from the same desire to be aggressively modern, regardless of congruity. These are all too apparent as we move along into Regent Street.

*Cintra House (right) and a detail of the façade (above).*

For example, Lloyds Bank at Hyde Park Corner could not present a more glaring contrast to the old and gentle commercial properties on the corner of Lensfield Road opposite. And further on, in St Andrew's Street, the former Belfast Linen Warehouse, now Wagamama and All Bar One, has an unredeemed vileness that is made worse by its contrast with the domestic scale and picturesque roofline of the Varsity restaurant. However did it get planning permission, even in the Brave New Sixties?

But it would turn this chapter into a gazetteer if one commented in detail on this long, dull stretch. The Hills Road approach is much as one would expect of any town. It begins well, then deteriorates into a nondescript high street for the last mile or so. Or it did until recently. Now we have the shocking blunders by the railway bridge and the insensitive vanity of Botanic House. These are what we have to fear most for the future; modern sensation-seeking stunts and metropolitan glitz.

*Ugly and overbearing, the Brutalist cube of the old Belfast Linen Warehouse rudely jostles the Varsity restaurant in St Andrew's Street.*

## The Hauxton Road / Trumpington Road approach

The southwestern approach has always been important, branching as it does from the Great North Road, and since the construction of the M11 it has assumed an even greater importance as an artery into the city. Shortly before entering Trumpington, the Hauxton Road used to display only one regrettable development, Bishop's Court, an ugly group of low flats like a chest of drawers. The road has now been opened up, with a superstore on the site of the old Plant Breeding Institute, a new road leading to Adden-brooke's guarded by a regiment of traffic lights and, on either side, the tightly packed dwellings of Trumpington Meadows and Great Kneighton that are springing up under the new Local Plan.

In contrast, the Trumpington Road part of the approach is remarkably good, apart from Trumpington village itself, whose high street was utterly wrecked in the 20th century, most strikingly by the fortress-like offices of Bidwells, an estate agent which specialises in fine country houses.

Leaving the village, the left-hand side of the road is miraculously devoid of housing, and beyond a narrow belt of trees the fields stretch away to Grantchester Meadows. A little further on, two prep schools occupy the grounds of former large houses. The first of these, The Perse Preparatory School, has built an unsympathetic and large modern classroom block alongside the Gothic Revival Leighton House, and its stark black and white

*The Hauxton Road / Trumpington Road approach, entering Cambridge from the southwest along the A1309.*

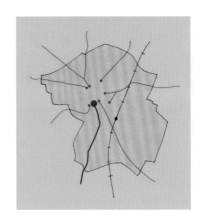

*A Grade II listed building on Trumpington High Street.*

rectilinear form interrupts an otherwise pleasant view. Luckily it is screened by trees in the summer. The buildings of St Faith's Preparatory School are mostly invisible, but this happy circumstance is negated by rather intrusive and excessive signage; surely one sign at the main entrance would do. Between the two schools lie the Trinity College developments of Porson, Barrow and Bentley roads, whose houses are so aligned that their gable ends, gardens and trees provide the frontage to Trumpington Road, thus minimising the appearance of ribbon development. Older houses on the other side of the road stand in gardens of a size and seclusion as to maintain the *rus in urbe* feel.

*The monolithic Bidwells building - the largest structure on the High Street - exhibits all the friendliness, charm and grace of a Norman keep*

While mature trees line the road on both sides up to Coe Fen and the Botanic Garden, helpfully screening the one or two examples of garden-grabbing developments and flats, a forest of traffic lights at the junction of Brooklands Avenue makes one wish for the extermination of the motor car. Compare this to the pastoral scene of sheep being driven along by this spot, with Downing College visible across the fields, in the print of 1809 entitled 'Cambridge from the first milestone'. On the right, past the Botanic Garden, Brookside stands gaunt but set back behind the delightful, tree-shaded Hobson's Brook. A fence and trees similarly conceal some of the mishmash development around The Leys' playing field, a hopelessly uncoordinated jumble of styles. Then we are into Trumpington Street and the urban centre, after a mile-long welcome from trees, like a guard of honour.

Trumpington Street itself, right through to King's Parade, is an extraordinary vista with scarcely a jolt – almost as perfect as a street could be. It would be a dereliction of our duty to posterity if this approach to Cambridge were not preserved.

*The urban and the pastoral clash at the junction of Brooklands Avenue and Trumpington Road.*

*The near-perfect Trumpington Street.*

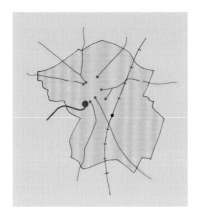

*The Barton Road approach, entering Cambridge from the west along the A603.*

*The rotunda of the Chancellor's Centre, Wolfson College, which gives an uncomfortable impression of trying too hard.*

## The Barton Road approach

This approach is protected by the relative absence of development on the west side of Cambridge – so far. If the view from the Gogs gives the best overall vantage point, this approach is the best from the flat ground, showing as it does a low-level horizon with little punctuation.

From the bridge over the motorway, St John's Chapel tower, King's Chapel, the University Library and the Catholic Church provide a modest but inviting indication of the distant city.

The intrusion of Carter Bridge into the skyline is slightly regrettable, but the utility of the bridge to cyclists and pedestrians is so important that it tempers one's vexation. The Chemistry buildings in Lensfield Road show up more than one would wish, as do the white-topped blocks of flats in the station Triangle. Further round is the inescapable sight of Addenbrooke's, probably visible from Mars. But it could be much worse. This is a skyline to be preserved.

It might be argued that so level a skyline would benefit from a few more 'landmark' buildings. Maybe it would, but not if The Marque is anything to go by. Such thinking is fraught with risks, and a temptation to be avoided. Tall buildings need a worthy purpose; otherwise they are no more than boastful towers showing that the ancient practice of phallic worship has not died out, as all too many cities demonstrate. Those that have gone for skyscrapers utterly forget any sense of hierarchy, without which the skyline degenerates into anarchy. Our sense of propriety usually tells us that a bank should not dwarf a cathedral. Cambridge should resist the intrusion of vulgar show-offs.

The view from further on has been obliterated by a fairly dense belt of trees to the south of the road, planted some twenty years ago. Then we are into a leafy avenue of substantial and inoffensive houses and the equally tame buildings of Wolfson College. The college's newer additions use good materials and finish but have an air about them of trying too hard. This is especially true of the Chancellor's Centre with its shiny, uncoloured metal coat of arms and its rotunda-like and lantern structures.

To our right, on the other side of the road, numbers 49-51 in front of Archway Court are the first to catch the eye. The three-storey section attracts by its neat proportions, pale blue shutters and primrose-painted brick. The pink doors, with porthole windows on either side, are suitably pastel. A modern arch connects to a later block in white. A distinctive feature is the pine tree in front, whose pale blue-green perfectly complements the blue shutters. As long as the tree remains, these houses could not sensibly be any other colour.

Further on, beyond the former Hat and Feathers pub, we see Ashworth Park, a dull new block of flats entirely without quietness or distinction. It possesses some pseudo-Victorian elements in its gables and rounded (artificial) slates, but it has neither Victorian exuberance nor Arts and Crafts verve, nor Modernist simplicity. The obligatory iron bars appear across the inward-opening 'French windows' which allow residents to gain maximum benefit from traffic noise without falling out. These contrivances give an uneasy suggestion of prison bars.

Still focusing on the south (right-hand) side of the road, which contains the most interesting buildings, we pass a pair of tall, gaunt and pretentious Victorian red- and yellow-brick houses. The left-hand example, helpfully named 'The Red House', is particularly pompous, boasting a wealth of mock-baronial detailing and a cupola precariously perched on one flank like an afterthought (see p. 34). But then we come to Croft Gardens, a more agreeably eye-catching development, symmetrical, beautifully composed, with pale green roof tiles and a well-judged massing of ridge roofs, hipped roofs and chimneys.

It forms a three-sided court in which cone-shaped yews are grouped. Art Deco influence is apparent in the door canopies and the moulded lines between the ground and first floors, and the pale green balcony rails harmonise perfectly with the roof tiles. In two respects, however, its buildings have been disappointingly modified.

*Croft Gardens.*

Firstly, the stucco walls have been changed from white to a less convincing cream, and secondly the replacement doors and windows do not respect the original conception, an all-too-common error. It is worth comparing the fenestration of its contemporary, Maitland House, a little further on.

*The Red House - rampant ostentation from an earlier age.*

*Maitland House.*

Maitland House (1937) is a very attractive white Art Deco construction, and one of the most memorable buildings on this road. While similar to Croft Gardens, it retains its original windows whose glazing bars, also found in the doors, increase the horizontal emphasis. It is a pity that the original green painted frames have been changed to a less authentic black, and regrettable, too, that the trees in front are ill chosen. A tall chestnut, a new cherry tree and a scraggy, faded fir fail to harmonise with each other and do nothing to complement the building behind them. The fir in particular is quite awful and should be felled. Yew topiary, as at Croft Gardens, would look well here.

The road turns at this point and becomes Newnham Road, which runs on to Queens' Road and the Backs. The charming Perse almshouses of 1886 have a hideous petrol station as their neighbour, a very unfortunate juxta-position. Causewayside, an apartment block on the north side of the Fen Causeway, is not wholly unpleasant, though its white-painted bays catch the attention more than they should.

The terrace and row of shops beyond the garage are currently being redeveloped by Clare College into 32 'student residential units', and while their frontages are to be left intact, the human-scale charm of Newnham Road will almost certainly not survive. Passing them, we reach the turn where, behind its mellow wall, the Malting House stands – an early 19th-century oast house rebuilt before the start of the First World War, and now owned by Darwin College. Then comes Silver Street on our right, Queens' Road straight ahead, and with it the start of the Backs.

This is another attractive approach, though vulnerable to new housing development from the north side towards Madingley Road. Proposed by the Holford Report sixty years ago, such intensification would have an unpleasant impact if ever revived.

*Clockwise from top left: the Perse Almshouses and lurid petrol station, Causewayside, the Malting House, and Newnham Road prior to redevelopment.*

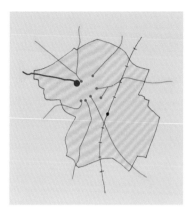

*The Madingley Road approach, entering Cambridge from the west along the A1303.*

## The Madingley Road approach

This is another western approach, also tree-lined as it runs towards the north end of the Backs, but being eroded at the outer approaches by the university's West Site development. Clerk Maxwell Road and J.J. Thomson Avenue lead off to the south into the former fields. The impression here, in winter, is that of a bleak new Danish suburb, neat and tidy but rather soulless at present. In summer the trees screen much. Tower blocks of moderate height have been introduced, and some of the buildings run close to the category of 'sensation-seeking stunts'. They are a little way off the road, however, and need not draw the eye if one is determined.

Further on, Churchill College has planted new trees inside its boundary. Together with the earlier trees by the roadside, they give a double screen against the sight and sound of traffic and enhance the sense of green enclosure along what would otherwise be a rather nakedly open site.

The opposite side of the road presents the kind of inappropriate infill that often occurs in otherwise harmonious roads. The preposterously named Blenheim Court, a dull building in red brick, stands perched above garages, with a nasty waste of tarmac in front.

*J.J. Thomson Avenue, looking towards the West Site development.*

*Churchill Court, with its abandoned
bed springs, and Blenheim Court in the
background.*

Beside it, the newer Churchill Court, built in 2005, is a fine example of Anytown architecture; there must be pattern books from which such designs are selected. As one comes along from the west, its white cubes catch the eye like a blemish and, from close up, one can see the obligatory metal balconies, fussy and rather industrial. On the front lawn there is a modern 'sculpture' of predictable silliness – a representation of half a globe but looking more like a nest of crumpled bedsprings. There are doubtless symbolic references one could speculate about, or invent, but such scrap-metal 'installations' seem horribly dated and clichéd, and intrinsically without meaning.

On the corner of Wilberforce Road is a block that could be taken for council maisonettes on any estate in the land. This is not to say that all council estates are architecturally inferior, nor should they be; but it is a sad fact that many of them are. In contrast, by the corner of Grange Road, stands a very attractive, neat new red-brick house. It has the quiet, unostentatious dignity of a home of real distinction and, unlike the would-be-smart Churchill Court, blends in well with the older setting.

A short distance on and we are at the north end of the Backs, having followed a leafy avenue almost as impressive as the approach along Trumpington Road. Our next approach is a different matter.

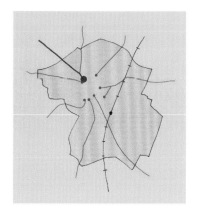

*The Huntingdon Road approach, entering Cambridge from the northwest along the A1307.*

*Castle Park, on the corner of Huntingdon Road and Victoria Road - meretricious buildings of baffling silliness.*

## The Huntingdon Road approach

For millennia this has been the major route in and out of Cambridge. Some hundred years ago, before the advent of motor traffic, it was a bleak, empty road with scarcely a house between Fenstanton and Girton. Today there is ribbon development from Girton into the town, with the former NIAB site turning into a housing estate of predictable density. However, the road has trees and is lined with substantial houses in large gardens until it reaches the warren of small streets opposite Fitzwilliam College. Then things go downhill in every sense.

Looming ahead is the busy junction with Histon Road, Victoria Road and Mount Pleasant. Such traffic nightmares are an inescapable part of almost any approach to a town. It is not so much the traffic – though that is bad enough – as the means of accommodating and directing it that produce such visually depressing results. Thus we have a small prairie of tarmac with painted markings, bollards, direction signs, traffic lights, and those insulting metal barriers designed either to stop pedestrians from flinging themselves into the road or cars from mounting the pavement as they cut corners – neither of them very likely eventualities.

The pedestrian, when the lights eventually permit him to cross, has to negotiate a labyrinth of railings rather than taking the natural direct route, a kind of 'chicanery' found all too often in our streets.

That is unfortunate enough. But what is more regrettable is that the buildings, which here on Castle Hill should be announcing one's arrival into the ancient heart of the city, are so phenomenally dull. This has long been an undistinguished area and its redevelopment since the 1970s has made no difference. The motorist waiting at the lights is confronted on the left by the Castle Park development, a place with one of those names bearing no relation to observable reality – there is no park here and the castle was demolished several hundred years ago – and on the right by an earlier office block with the risible name of Mount Pleasant House. Although this one does refer to an adjacent real street, the view is anything but pleasant.

Mount Pleasant House was built in 1979 on land left derelict for many years. One thing to be said in its favour is that the De Vere Hotel originally proposed for the site would have been much worse. That was to have been the biggest hotel in East Anglia and it would also have been the biggest eyesore.

The present office block is not so shocking but it suffers from the disease of so many modern buildings, obesity. Building to a human scale has long since given way before the imperative of profit: 'pile them high'. How much can be fitted onto the site? How high will we be allowed to build? What is the maximum we can get away with? These seem to be the questions of most concern to developers. But how many of them know beforehand who will want to locate to their offices? The long-empty mistake by Hills Road bridge answers that. Yet they are quick to suggest at any time that there is a 'desperate need' for office accommodation.

Mount Pleasant House is accordingly a large development and has been angled zigzag fashion to reduce its impact and to turn the corner. There is a basement car park screened by trees and shrubs, gloomy but at least green. The façade is relentlessly horizontal, with four bands of glass between four bands of brick, entirely unrelieved by any verticals. The result is like a pile of false teeth. It looms threateningly above Shelly Row, which looks as if it is about to be eaten.

*The grinning dentures of Mount Pleasant House menace Shelly Row.*

*Shelly Garden looking gappy and incomplete.*

Over the road, Shelly Garden has its moments, but it is the irritating oddities that draw the eye. The corner makes a fussy attempt at novelty with its two circular windows unmatched by any other circular or curved forms. Instead there are angular cutaways giving access and light to staircases, creating the unsettling effect of a drawer that has been left open; one wants to push it shut. The long façade has blank, gappy openings and a barred section in the centre of the top floor, giving the impression that it is a multistorey car park.

Looking back to the junction with Histon Road, we are confronted by what architects in 2009 voted as one of the city's 'worst eyesores', though there are plenty of candidates for that title. The former Texaco garage site would not be on any tourist trail, but the would-be developers, Cambridge Land Limited, are keen to make the most of its aesthetic deficiencies in order to justify their own proposals. They have decided that 'student' accommodation would be a good wheeze, provoking concerns about what sort of students. Unsurprisingly they want a four-storey building. Their first design was rejected by the City Council planners as 'mediocre', an action one would think was justified in a good many more cases too. The revised design, submitted in August 2011, has allegedly been simplified into a 'well-ordered piece of architecture, with use of traditional high quality materials', and the removal of 'inappropriate materials' (these are the developer's words).

One has to ask why an 'inappropriate' and disordered design was submitted in the first place. In November 2011 the revised plan was also rejected. We awaited the outcome with no high hopes and the development was allowed on appeal. Currently the corner is pleasantly open to the sky, which will not be the case when the approved four-storey block goes up.

On the other side of the road lies Castle Park, the most visually disastrous of the new developments in this area so far. One would almost welcome the return of the former miscellany of temporary, low, flat-roofed, boxy offices, huts, sheds and wire-mesh fencing. Then, there were at least a few trees and some open space. Now the site has been intensively developed and in a most peculiar style. It displays some consistency but the resemblance to Milton Keynes or Reading is inescapable and unwelcome. Even more than Mount Pleasant House, this is a large, monotonously uniform development. Built in the 1980s, it is very much a period piece. Not for the last time we see the trick of using a contrast on the top storey to try to disguise the fact that these buildings are a floor higher than their neighbours. In this case it does not work. The band of uninterrupted windows is topped by a dark pitched roof which negates the attempt to lighten the top storey. Worse, the clean lines are broken by bizarrely curved dormer-like tops to the stair wells. They

*The old Texaco Garage site, allegedly one of the worst eyesores in Cambridge, nonetheless does not loom as large as its proposed replacement.*

seem to have no practical function, and the buildings would be better without them. The junction of the two ranges by Victoria Road would have been the place to give relief to the horizontal lines, but instead of a solid vertical we find a void, a cavity partly filled with glass (see photo on p. 39). If a tower is wanted, let it be a real one, and not a half-hearted pile of greenhouses.

Further along, the curved hood motif becomes even more preposterous in the form of two feeble towers or pillars a bit like giant gateposts. They appear to mark an entrance which is yet blocked by the peculiar survival of Allways House, a pleasant but unexceptional Victorian building now caught like a prisoner between aliens. Why does it remain, when other such structures are regularly demolished without demur? What, one wonders, thwarted the developers? Less mysterious is the reason for the ubiquitous 'hoodie'; above the gable of the Sir Isaac Newton pub is a curved pediment slightly bigger than a semicircle, a feature that the architects of Castle Park have latched onto and repeated *ad nauseam*. It is the sole extent of their deference to pre-existing buildings.

*Above and facing page: Castle Park mindlessly repeats its banal reference to one single feature of a pre-existing building.*

*Castle Court - a fish tank perched on a greenhouse.*

*An unexpected survival: Allways House dwarfed by alien structures.*

Beyond the pub, it is a relief to return to two-storey buildings for a short stretch, and St John's Chapel tower beckons from the bottom of the hill. There is an example of good redevelopment on the left, in the rather fancifully named King's Keep (see photo overleaf). This is a very welcome addition to the street scene. Its materials blend well with the surroundings, and the four-storey height is ameliorated by the falling gradient of the road. The cylindrical corner tower is easy on the eye, while its top balcony grows naturally from the building. It makes good use of its position, nicely poised near the crest and turn of the hill, and the small tower provides a focus to the approach from the Histon Road corner. Only on the south façade is the effect marred by cream stucco, which weakens the allusion to a fortress and disturbs the overall harmony of the building. Nonetheless, this scores high marks.

Further down looms a far less successful attempt to fit in. The steep-pitched gables and feeble details of St Giles Court, built in 1986, ape the older row of four houses beyond it. This latter Victorian terrace is well composed, the doors and bays neatly grouped, the details nicely judged and the effect quietly distinguished. In its time, features like the red pilasters at the ends might have been seen as pretentious decoration, yet beside its modern neighbour it cuts a far finer figure.

*The King's Keep.*

The chief feature of St Giles Court is its all-too-familiar obesity. It is like an inflated semidetached house, its proportions too large, its roof too heavy, its windows too big, its bays too flat. The architects have tried to make it blend in, but their response to their brief has produced a design that is predictably out of scale.

*Left to right: St Giles Court and its Victorian neighbour.*

Magdalene College, with the bridge just ahead, signals the end of this approach.

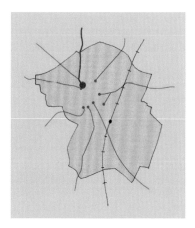

*The Histon Road approach, entering Cambridge from the north along the B1049.*

## The Histon Road approach

Since the construction of the A14 in the 1970s, Histon Road has become a more important route into the city. Coming down from the flyover one has a view on the right of open fields, suggesting how rural this spot felt until quite recently. On the left is a panoramic view of Orchard Park that is not encouraging: to see homes pressed up right against the A14, requiring a wall to shield them (inadequately) from the incessant traffic noise, instantly provokes the wish that the planners who thought this was a beneficent act should be compelled to live there. (The Orchard Park development is further discussed in Chapter 13.)

Then comes the large junction with King's Hedges Road, a vast expanse of tarmac and lights to cope with the volume of traffic generated by the new development. This horrid junction, and the rabbit warrens of Orchard Park pressed up against the A14, exemplify the depressing visual squalor and overcrowding that now characterises the edges of so many towns.

Beyond the junction the view improves considerably. Parts of the old hedgerows remain, with mature trees augmented by later planting, all of which softens and screens the suburban development that has taken place here in the last thirty to forty years. This consists of solid, quiet,

*Histon Road at the junction of King's Hedges Road - the trees remind us that not so long ago this was little more than a country lane.*

*Competing shop signs near the junction with Windsor Road hurl violent primary colours at passers-by.*

*Two newly built homes harmoniously inserted into a Victorian terrace - a welcome example of respect for the character of neighbouring buildings.*

*Histon Road Cemetery lodge.*

unpretentious houses, maisonettes and flats. Mostly two storey, they are thoughtfully aligned at ninety degrees to the road, which minimises their visual impact and spares their residents, as far as possible, from traffic noise. This leafy and pleasant state of affairs continues as far as the Gilbert Road junction, at which point older ribbon development takes over, interspersed with in-your-face garages, car and motorcycle showrooms and a shabby parade of shops defaced by hideous signage. Only the cemetery, with its mock Elizabethan Tudor lodge, provides anything worth noticing; the building is actually recorded and pictured in volume two of the survey of Cambridge by the Royal Commission on Historical Monuments (1959).

On the corner of Akeman Street a short terrace of council houses has been demolished, and a block of 14 apartments (all but three of which are single-bed flats) is going up in its place. It is a sign of the times that council housing can be sold off to developers, whose aim is not to give people decent houses with gardens but to make maximum profit by cramming onto a site as many 'residential units' as the law or planners will allow.

Two recent sites on this road exemplify two current trends in urban redevelopment. Firstly, on the west side towards the top of the hill stands Richard Newcombe Court (2011), a smart contemporary apartment block possessed of several clichés that will date very quickly: timber cladding, white render, metal railings and balconies. It also bears the inevitable signs announcing that it is 'guarded' by CCTV. Secondly, standing directly opposite the cemetery lodge, a pair of excellent new houses (shown on p. 48) fit perfectly into the 19th-century terrace. They could be accused of pastiche but it might be better to say that they adopt the style of their neighbours. The result is certainly very satisfactory, which cannot always be said of blatant modernity in an older setting.

As one nears the junction with Victoria Road, the ghastly sight of Mount Pleasant House cuts across the horizon. Welcome to Cambridge.

*The southern end of Histon Road, looking towards the junction with Victoria Road and Mount Pleasant.*

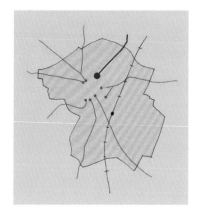

*The Milton Road approach, entering Cambridge from the northeast along the A1309.*

## The Milton Road approach

Fifty years ago, this 18th-century road from Ely passed through bare country, then came to derelict land before entering a leafy suburban road. It is a striking feature of old photographs how well furnished such roads were with trees.

Crossing the A14 today, the traveller sees St John's Innovation Park on the left and Trinity Science Park on the right. Both college enterprises have tidied up old ground – the latter was once a tank training area and is now filled with futuristic buildings, much glass, and odd shapes that will date more quickly than less ostentatious ones. Large modern structures such as these often have cluttered skylines, with roofs sporting lift shafts, vents, solar panels and mobile phone masts. They are irritatingly untidy, like unfinished Greek houses with steel rods protruding from the concrete.

*First impressions of Cambridge from Milton Road - the Edinburgh Building on St John's Innovation Park, right, and the Philips Research Building on the Trinity Science Park, below.*

*Left and facing page: Byron House, The Golden Hind and Citygate - all buildings on Milton Road that show the attractive possibilities of the pitched roof.*

Coming down from the flyover we see Byron House ahead of us, showing an attractive grouping of pitched roofs which makes a neat composition against the curve of the road. Ignoring the predictable car showroom/garage on the right we are into tree-lined suburbia.

There are some interesting eye-catchers here and there, like the Golden Hind pub (1937), all gables and chimneys like sticks of barley sugar. Its composition seen from the corner of Green End Road is particularly effective. It is not a listed building, but it ought to be.

Further on, by Woodhead Drive, stands Citygate, a newly built Voysey-esque apartment block in pale yellow brick, with dark green window frames and a beautifully pitched roof in dark grey artificial slate. The bays are 'tile' hung in the same material. The stairwell has fenestration more akin to Art Deco, but overall this is a striking and well-proportioned building.

There are also occasional mild horrors, like the 1930s parade of shops between Union Lane and Highworth Avenue, flat-roofed and looking very shabby now, though doubtless considered smart and up-to-the-minute when built. And on the corner of Hurst Park Avenue is Dalegarth, a dull block of flats dating from 1964, its cuboid lines clashing with the pitched roofs of the older houses opposite.

*The shopping parade between Union Lane and Highworth Avenue - modest inter-war Modernism in a suburban setting.*

Finally, as we approach Gilbert Road, the Cambridge Manor Care Home makes itself glaringly conspicuous while performing the usual stunts in an effort to conceal its size and bulk. The corner façade is clad in timber planks, giving it a temporary look, as of a packing case. Further along, the surface becomes off-white render, then yellow brick, and the top floor employs the 'concealment' device of being in a different colour, this time dark grey rather than white to blend in with leaden skies.

*The Cambridge Manor Care Home on Milton Road - out of place, out of scale and out of sympathy with its surroundings.*

All this succeeds in breaking up the large façade but results in a jumble rather than attractive variety. Differences of height, colour and texture work better when they are accidental, as in King's Parade; they are not so easy to contrive deliberately, and less so when attempting to minimise what we can all see is a single large plane. This high-impact building will not be alone; more development is expected on this site of a former primary school.

Very soon we are at Mitcham's Corner and near the main crossing of the Cam. Overall it is not a bad entrance to Cambridge.

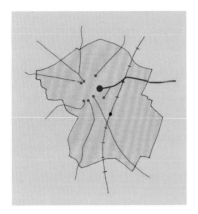

*The Newmarket Road approach, entering Cambridge from the east along the A1303 and A1134.*

## The Newmarket Road approach

On this approach, the first sight of the city comes about a mile west of Quy. From the roundabout at Airport Way, we see Marshall's airfield and, on the skyline, the inescapable tower and buildings of Addenbrooke's Hospital. Ahead is the Newmarket Road Park and Ride sign, with the car park on the right well concealed behind a stand of trees. Opposite, Marshall's has thoughtfully planted trees in front of its airport buildings, but there is no getting away from the cluster of a dozen traffic-light posts, street lamps and pedestrian barriers that mark the entrance to the site.

Marshall's old airport buildings are rather pleasant and simple, exemplifying inter-war Art Deco notions of streamlined modernity and having none of the larger ostentation we might expect today. That is to be seen in the lurid Shell garage on the right, soon followed by a parade of car showrooms where ranks of stationary cars look out at ranks of passing cars, the most defining objects of our time.

The typical suburban stretch which follows, belonging to the Whitehills estate, is made less dull for a while by the mature trees of the city cemetery. Beyond them, at the corner of Ditton Lane, stands Lothbury House, part of an investment company's portfolio. This office block remained empty and unused for nearly two decades, presumably generating capital all by itself, and has only recently been put to proper use and leased to tenants once more. Particularly drab suburbia opens up between here and the Barnwell Road roundabout, until the road begins to drop as it passes the Abbey football stadium and a tiny portion of Coldham's Common on the left.

*Stylish inter-war design at Marshall's Airport.*

On our right, in quick succession, are four much older buildings of some historic interest. The first of these is the former Globe Inn, which abuts at right angles onto the second, a picturesque house once known as 'The Moat' and before that as 'Paper Mills' – and indeed paper was made on this site in the 16th century. The former inn is a sorry shadow of what it once was, given over now to a restaurant, a takeaway and a betting shop. Each has made its disfiguring marks on the once handsome building, with corporate tagging and primary colours taking predictable priority, though one is not aware of any law requiring commercial signs to be lurid. (One feels that an education in graphics and aesthetics would make a welcome addition to the school curriculum.) The garden wall of The Moat, shaded by trees, runs down to the third historic building, an interesting old turnpike toll house called The Round House. Beyond that is the Norman Leper Chapel, a reminder that this was once an out-of-the-way place.

*Top: Indecently exposed vehicles solicit the attention of passing motorists.*

*Centre: The Round House.*

*Bottom: Paper Mills.*

On the crest of the rise ahead looms Signet Court, a fairly well-proportioned 1980s building whose rooflines respect those of the terraced houses beyond. We are now coming into Barnwell and the old industrial part of Cambridge, once the site of brick kilns, railway yards and gasworks. Today it is given over to large retail units with strident signs and colours. It is a pity these places must solicit for custom so blatantly, dressed in the building equivalent of fishnet tights and scarlet nail varnish.

*The former Globe Inn.*

Ahead of us, on the right, is the former Comet warehouse, a very presentable building in patterned brick, its façade broken by shallow piers like pilasters or buttresses. Only the inevitably loud signage spoils it. On our left are the smart, carefully designed, well-balanced buildings of Newmarket Road Retail Park. If we must have mega-stores, the composition of these is better than many. Further on down the road, more flashy signs shout for attention, forgetting that when everything is triple *forte* one quickly becomes deaf. Once past them, we come to the junction with Coldhams Lane.

*Warehouses do not have to be dull or ugly, as this example shows.*

When this book was begun, the Coldhams Lane junction was an atrociously depressing corner, home to the boxy crates of Intercell House. This has now been demolished to make way for a six-storey, 121-room budget hotel, which however inflated, mediocre or cliché ridden it proves to be, could not possibly be as utterly repellent as its predecessor. On the other side of Coldham's Lane another budget hotel has just been completed. Resembling a stack of giant date boxes, the six-storey 219-bed Travelodge Eastern Gate Hotel is vast, possessing the dimensions of a cruise liner. Its height and great length, dispiritingly visible from several miles away, create yet another conspicuous intrusion above the Cambridge skyline.

*A shipyard on Newmarket Road - the S S Travelodge under construction in January 2013 (above), and completed in June 2013.*

It will not be long, perhaps, before the other side of the road is redeveloped, and the result will almost certainly be a canyon of tall buildings. Meanwhile, go and look while you can at J.H. Cooper and Son, a rare historic survival of commercial premises unchanged for over half a century.

Beyond the hotel runs a long wall, for maybe 200 yards; not a pleasant wall nodding with trees but the windowless back of the Eastern Court business park, covered in very low grade graffiti. It is a sight of depressing offensiveness and a disgrace to Cambridge.

This is the kind of thing one would normally paint over instantly in order to demoralise the vandals, who see their laborious efforts erased in minutes. So what is going on here? Do the owners have an interest in seeing their buildings degraded? It would appear that they do. A plaque states that the 'artwork' is by 'Blight Society' (that says it all), with the permission of Eastern Gate Property Ltd. Presumably its purpose was to turn a dull wall into something so offensive that local residents would welcome its demolition and greet any new building, however overbearing, with cries of joy and relief.

*Above: Society blighted by Blight Society - vile, suicide-inducing imagery on the walls of the Eastern Court business park.*

*Right: A rare historic survival - J.H. Cooper's furniture store still trading in its original warehouse.*

Further on, we see the vast roundabout at Elizabeth Way/East Road. To our right as we approach it stands the 13th-century Abbey Church of St Andrew the Less, hidden by leaves in summer. The unspeakably dull office cube next to it, fittingly called 'Logic House', could not offer a more dreary contrast to the medieval imagination. Then follows a brief run of human-scale Victorian shops and houses, which soon gives way to the roundabout.

The area here is largely a mess, as traffic-relieving schemes tend to be – elegant on plan, vile on the ground. Visual dislocation is caused by the opening up of a wide expanse that lacks an obvious focus. The trees in the central circle, welcome though they are for their greenery, block the view ahead to where the road continues into town. The motorist is therefore at the mercy of signs. The widely spaced buildings show no coherence in the way they face the roundabout, and the confusion is compounded by the old line of Occupation Road, cut off when the new route was built in 1971, but still visible. National Tyre and Autocare displays all the stridency of signage one expects of such a service. Cambridge Riverside (see Chapter 8) stands behind it. Compass House on the East Road side, partly screened by trees, has neat brickwork but an odd angular stance to the curve of the road. The usual railings imprison pedestrians, though some will prefer to sprint across the road rather than take the detour into the noisome pedestrian subway.

*Logic House - a shoe box on stilts.*

*'Now what?' asks a perplexed cyclist, confronted by a blank wall where he might reasonably expect to find a sign. Unfortunately for him, the Elizabeth Way subway system is a signage-free zone.*

*Left: Cliché-ridden Cambridge Riverside on Newmarket Road.*

*Below: A flavour of Soviet-era East Berlin - the pedestrian subway at Elizabeth Way roundabout.*

The subway opens into a sad, neglected apology for a garden. A peculiar 'sculpture' of lamps – looking like blighted trees – has been rendered more risible by being made to bear an aerial and a CCTV camera. The exit tunnels have no street names and the buildings above can hardly be seen; you need to have checked your bearings quite carefully if you hope to emerge where you intended. But then who cared about pedestrians in the futuristic 1960s? After all, everyone would soon be flying around with jet packs on their backs.

From the roundabout there are two routes into the city centre: a left turn takes you into East Road, while straight ahead, Newmarket Road runs into Maids' Causeway and Jesus Lane. At the start of this stretch a homely pub, The Brunswick Arms, is now lost amongst a jumble of newer buildings – the tyre place, lawyers' dull offices and the smart new Cambridge Riverside apartments. This latter development suffers from a number of currently fashionable clichés; its light brick is augmented by blond wood and an area of white stucco for contrast, while the obligatory balconies have railings rather too similar to those used for fencing in pedestrians at junctions; the word 'cage' comes readily to mind.

Opposite stands the banal three-storey range of Dukes Court (1988) and a row of assorted 20th-century buildings. This short stretch of road, also known as Sun Street, has always had its building line set back, and this, along with its present stylistic incoherence, creates an unsettling, untidy effect that makes one glad to get away. It is therefore a relief to reach Maids' Causeway and a properly tree-lined avenue of clear structure.

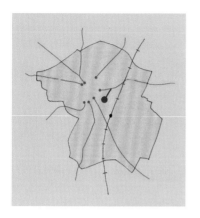

*The East Road approach, along the A603, branches off from Newmarket Road.*

## The East Road approach

Turning left at Elizabeth Way roundabout brings us into East Road, where New Vile competes with Old Vile for supremacy. On our left, uninspiring flats are followed by Mackay's hardware store. The firm's first premises, Britannia House, are unexceptional and quiet enough, the original lettering above its windows a reminder of the possibilities of well-proportioned clarity. During the time this book was in preparation, it was obliterated by the large, loud, ugly signage that is all too common today in order to catch the eye of the onrushing motorist.

When it comes to maintaining the dignity of government or the law, tax-payers' money is freely spent, and the new Crown Court seems to have had plenty lavished upon it. It is not a bad design – curved brick walls lend a touch of class to any building – and its fortress-like appearance suits its function.

*Cambridge Crown Court.*

**63**

*Cambridge Working Men's Club.*

On the other side of the road stands the Cambridge Working Men's Club, a nicely proportioned building of neat brick with two courses of black brick between floors to provide contrast. The entrance is clearly and logically placed in the central angle of the two ranges, and all the lines are agreeably clean and sharp. Perhaps less successful is the panelling in imitation of half-timbering. The red pillars and lamp posts also jar but there are obvious political reasons for the choice of such a colour.

*The poky rear entrance to 'The Grafton'.*

Next comes the muddle that is the back of 'The Grafton' (whatever happened to 'Centre'?). British Home Stores feels it important to announce its presence in large letters high up on the building, but perhaps we should be grateful there is not a complete list of retailers there. The entrance is not very inviting; there is the bus dropping-off point and unaccountable openings that might or might not be roads to somewhere. The street scene is full of posts, bollards, bins, hopeless sculpture, uncertainty and those terrible utilitarian grey railings. One can only say, thank goodness for trees.

*Looking back in the direction we have come, we see Anglia Ruskin University (above), and the brown façade of Wellington House with the County Court beyond it (below).*

Beyond stands Abbeygate House, a peculiar building of unconvincing shape, short on bricks, big on glass and nasty brown panels. It displays quite ghastly signage in violent red and yellow, running all along the windows. Who thought that was a good idea? A little further on, beyond the junction of Norfolk Street and Burleigh Street, lies a short, run-down stretch of older properties, the garishly signed land of Tesco Express and KFC.

Past these shops, pretentious, dull neo-classical buildings lead the eye towards the trees of Parker's Piece and the elegant spire of the Catholic Church – or at least they used to; Parkside Place has now gone up overlooking the Piece, and its seven-storey tower competes with the natural focal point of the spire. Further along, the smart, streamlined county court portrays the present notion of being up-to-the-minute, while the dull brown cube of Wellington House – dwarfed on both sides by its 21st-century neighbours – exemplifies an earlier, less showy, striving for modernity.

To our the left, on the south side of the road, Anglia Ruskin University's Helmore Building is so bland it could be a shopping mall. The same cannot be said of its neighbour: those who like Victorian architecture will welcome the interesting massing and Romanesque details of the Zion Baptist Church, built in 1878 and now a listed building. It could so easily have fallen victim to road-widening schemes in less enlightened days.

At Parker's Piece we reach a location of great visual importance that has recently been 'transformed', i.e. spoilt, by the replacement of the old fire station with Parkside Place. This ill-judged tower block will be discussed in Chapter 14. Here we are at a major crossroads where East Road meets Mill Road, Gonville Place and Parkside, so it is no surprise to find the obligatory playpen railings, in this instance so badly sited that they reduce the footpath by a quarter. Why not put them in the road?

Of all the approaches to Cambridge this has to be the worst; avoid it at all costs.

*Light at the end of the tunnel - the approach to Parker's Piece prior to the construction of Parkside Place.*

**66**

**3**

# The city centre

*This chapter falls into two sections. The first considers the city centre's built environment with specific reference to street furniture and paving, shop façades and open spaces. The second examines a number of locations where architectural vandalism is threatened, or has already taken place.*

## The built environment

### Street furniture

At one time streets had little in them. In Victorian photographs small groups of children stand in the road to stare at the novelty of a camera. The delightful pen and ink drawings of C.G. Harper from the early years of the 20th century depict old gaffers having conversations in the middle of high streets. Little else is seen other than the buildings and the occasional wheeled vehicle.

Today, playing games in the street or taking photos from the middle of the road requires suicidal optimism. Cataracts of traffic make it difficult to find even the few seconds required to cross a road, assuming one can squeeze through the barriers of nose-to-tail kerbside parking. Cars have brought unprecedented mobility at the cost of thousands of killings and maimings annually and a visual squalor of depressing ubiquity. Most do not even look good now that safety features, or possibly fashion, render them as obese as some of their occupants. They fill streets everywhere with visual clutter.

The motor car is a costly and demanding machine. Not only must it occupy acres of space, it must also have powerful street lighting and plenty of signs telling it what to do and what not to do. The pre-motor car street scene had little in it except gas lamps. But with motor vehicles came street signs, traffic lights, bollards, bus stops, bus shelters, roundabouts and gallons of paint on the tarmac. It has been said that many of these signs could be removed with no perceptible effect on road safety, and that drivers can see most dangers for themselves. Granted, some warning signs might be necessary for exceptional hazards but who has time to read a cluster of them? However, the bureaucratic mind insists on every precaution and we are stuck with signage.

**67**

Paradoxically, this is even more evident in the heart of the city, where some degree of pedestrianisation has occurred. City centre streets in the 1960s were a nightmare of traffic congestion. Then came the idea of reclaiming them for human beings as pedestrians. Unfortunately, a total ban on motor traffic is not considered possible in the centre of Cambridge nor, it would seem, even desirable. Selected vehicles are allowed through, marshalled by a multiplicity of signs. Road congestion is thus replaced by signage congestion. If no traffic were permitted, all this ironmongery could be swept away, to the great benefit of the street scene.

The adjacent photo was taken on what is possibly the finest thoroughfare in Cambridge. All the way from the Botanic Garden to Bridge Street via Trumpington Street, King's Parade, Trinity Street and St John's Street, there is at first sight nothing to spoil the sense of harmony and beauty. By great good fortune, the arrangement of buildings and trees and the gentle curve of the road have resulted in something close to perfection. And as with the High Street at Oxford, one is therefore compelled to ask why motor traffic and its accompanying street furniture is allowed anywhere near this marvel.

Looking at the route from the far end, where Bridge Street meets St John's Street, one is confronted by an astonishing forest of posts, bollards and signs. If you approached this junction in a wheeled vehicle you would have to stop for some time to work out from the chaos of signs what you were allowed to do. This information overload is absurd: you are redundantly reminded to be considerate to pedestrians and not flatten them. As for pedestrians who reach the other side of the street without being hedgehogged, they will find the narrow pavement further reduced by bollards, presumably intended to stop cars from mounting the pavement – although only one side of the road is thus protected. Two even stand sentry at the entrance to the wholly pedestrianised Rose Crescent, lest deluded lorry drivers think to enter.

The amount of signage and information beggars belief. A lamp post by All Saints' Passage is disfigured by seven signs. Who reads them? One is reminded of Mr Pooter, in 'The Diary of a Nobody', whose pleasure in the possibilities of Pinkford's red enamel paint leads him from painting the flower pots to the coal scuttle, the maid's washstand and then the bath. One imagines a member of the council similarly casting around, looking for reasons to affix signs. An unadorned lamp post is naked and must have its fig leaf of signage.

*Facing Page*

*Top: Signs at the entrance to King's Parade.*

*Bottom: Signage overload - a Richardson Candle by All Saints Passage disfigured by no less than seven signs.*

*Right: Martian war machines stalk King's Parade.*

*Below: A fine view of the Old Schools.*

The worst atrocities have occurred in, of all places, King's Parade. The tourist attempting to photograph King's College has to be carefully positioned to avoid lamp posts, traffic signs, tourist attraction signposts and that more recent visual horror, the municipal surveillance mast.

But King's Parade has suffered most of all from inappropriate street lighting. There is some history to this, and it is instructive. In 1957 the council installed new lamps here, as well as on Trumpington Street, Trinity Street and St John's Street. These were the 'Richardson Candles', elegant tubular lanterns mounted either on fluted cast iron columns or, as in the narrow thoroughfare of Trinity Street, on the walls of buildings – an arrangement that not only spared pedestrians the potential collisions, dodgings and diversions that posts cause, but also achieved a welcome absence of clutter. After four decades, however, they began to fail, and for a long time the council could not settle on a new design. While its deliberations dragged on, the Candles were being replaced in an *ad hoc* fashion; in King's Parade, an entire row was supplanted by cheap, supposedly temporary lamps which soon leaned wonkily about the place, while in Trumpington Street, piecemeal substitution resulted in a muddle that is still visible today. Standing by the Fitzwilliam Museum it is possible to see:

an original Candle on its column, a modern black post, two types of green metal post with either long or short arms, a post-mounted bogus Victorian-style lantern in black, and a grey metal post with a black lantern on top – six different designs in the space of a hundred or so yards.

What is more, most of these designs are too tall for their location. They doubtless fulfil some requirement to illuminate the road for cars, but the streets here are mainly for pedestrians and cyclists, and do not need to be so broadly or so brashly lit.

For the council, finding a modern lamp that approached the Richardson Candle in elegance and subtlety of illumination proved to be a lengthy process. A new design was finally agreed upon in 2008, and the following year a number of D.W. Windsor lanterns were installed along King's Parade. Their success has been mixed. Though simple in design, they are also spindly and do not look quite right – there is something alien about them, a hint of the Martian locomotion machine as described in H.G. Wells' 'The War of the Worlds' (see photo on p. 69). Their peculiar appearance quickly earned them the popular nickname of 'the needles'.

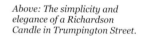

*Above: The simplicity and elegance of a Richardson Candle in Trumpington Street.*

*Left: Wall-mounted Richardson Candles eliminate street-level clutter in Trinity Street.*

*Facing Page*

*Top: The D.W. Windsor lanterns in operation on King's Parade, with a random sodium lamp in the background.*

*Bottom: An elegant sculptural bollard mutilated by an unnecessary sign.*

It should be possible to light these streets sympathetically and with a consistent design. In fact, the original solution is still the best: the bronze-coloured Richardson Candles are the right height, blend into the street scene, and provide perfectly adequate levels of illumination. English Heritage appears to agree, for in May 2011 it approved the Twentieth Century Society's application to have them Grade II listed. The programme of replacement with W.D. Windsor lanterns was duly abandoned, and most of the Candles that had fallen into disrepair over the years were restored to a semblance of their former glory. While this is a rare example of good sense and good taste triumphing over crass economics and cultural indifference, it does not address the ugliness caused by the miscellany of lamps that still remains along parts of this architecturally perfect thoroughfare.

In front of Great St Mary's, on Senate House Hill, we find a mixture of good intentions and startling unimaginativeness. This is a place where people congregate, but it does not say to us 'this is the place to stop'. It is too open to distracting movement, and wheeled traffic upsets any sense of repose – one is never quite safe from a bicycle or a reversing taxi. Nor is there anywhere comfortable to sit. There are benches, handsome ones, but without backs and set in the middle of the pavement where no one feels psychologically comfortable; none but the most leg-weary would enjoy sitting there for long. Several bollards direct the traffic. The elegant one shown left has had a 'cyclists keep left' sign crassly bolted onto it, a depressingly insensitive mutilation. 'Pooter-man' has been let loose again, like a child with a staple gun.

The man who invented traffic cones is said to have made a fortune. Whoever supplies Cambridge City Council with bollards must be similarly wealthy. The city centre bristles with them, herding pedestrians into narrow confines. People have to be constantly dodging these posts and each other, exactly what one does not want in a pedestrianised street. Could we hope that the health-and-safety nit-pickers might recognise the hazards and arrange for the removal of these obstacle courses?

King's Parade is not, of course, properly pedestrianised. Priority is still given to cars and parking, and cars take up a disproportionate amount of space in the street. Bollards march all the way down the pavement, further reducing pedestrian comfort.

The entrance to King's Parade at the junction with Silver Street would be the proper place for all those breeding bollards; put a nice row across to stop vehicles encroaching on this architectural wonder and you would not need to disfigure it with 'keep out' signs.

## Paving

Cambridge maybe a boom town but its streets are paved with gum. Before we ever notice the paving stones themselves, we see blackened pancakes of it augmented by cigarette ends, wine spills, phlegm expectorations and dried vomit, a testimony to the bestial habits of some of our less disciplined residents. The council does clean this up from time to time – though it is a labour of Sisyphus – and has also attempted, over the years, to make improvements to the quality of the street paving. Regrettably, its efforts in this direction have produced two problems; inconsistency of design and damage from heavy vehicles. Both proceed from a policy of half-hearted pedestrianisation. The first attempts saw pink bricks painstakingly laid on a bed of sand in St Andrew's Street, Sidney Street, St John's Street, Trinity

*Below: Cobbles in Green Street, and paving bricks being laid in St Andrew's Street .*

*Above: Paving in Sidney Street patched with tarmac - the consequence of damage by delivery vehicles.*

*Below: The paved main street of Hjørring in Denmark.*

Street and Market Street. In places where the foundations were uneven, they were dislodged in no time at all by the weight of lorries and buses that still had to pass through.

Sometimes they were replaced, sometimes they were patched with tarmac. The paving slabs on either side of the roadway were also cracked by heavy vehicles and repaired in the same way (as shown left). In 1999, twee cobbles were introduced in Green Street and part of King's Parade. They look picturesque but are hell to walk on, let alone cycle over or negotiate in a wheelchair. They are a daily reminder that we should be looking at ways to resurface our historic streets with attractive, good quality materials without sacrificing comfort or practicality.

If lorries and buses are to be allowed through 'pedestrianised' streets, the road surfaces should be treated accordingly, and that means tarmac – which need not look ugly – or extremely securely laid cobbles or sets. Conventional paving stones will not do in any area where a lorry may be allowed to park and unload; a pavement of broken slabs is unsightly, hazardous and a waste of money. The Danes, of course, have a solution to this. The main street of Hjørring has a winding strip of tarmac to which vehicles are confined. It supports their weight better than bricks or slabs, while the curving line adds interest and makes it harder for the impatient motorist to put his foot down. The carefully patterned stones are left untouched. In Cambridge, the tarmac could widen into loading bays where necessary.

It is encouraging to see that the council is intending to rejuvenate Fitzroy Street and Burleigh Street to give them a more consistent and less cluttered look, with repairs to the street surfaces. Some of the ugly tarmac patching in the city centre has also been replaced by appropriate paving; perhaps some of the clutter could go too, when funds permit.

## Shop façades

It is said that a good thing advertises itself. Retailers don't always like to take a chance on that; they try to make sure that their shops stand out. The results often compromise or destroy the integrity of the building and there is too frequently a glaring disjunction between the appearance of the ground floor and that of the floors above.

Cambridge city centre, full of listed buildings, has avoided some of the worst horrors of High Street blight; old-established independent shops like Ryder and Amies, Arthur Shepherd, Brian Jordan and G. David have maintained dignified frontages.

But the centre has not escaped the infiltration of chain stores – indeed in 2010 the New Economic Foundation named Cambridge Britain's pre-eminent 'clone town'. Corporate tagging appears even on shop fronts that are otherwise preserved, with the worst offenders making no reference at all to their upper storeys. It is like compelling a man in evening dress to wear pink wellingtons. One aspect of this is structural, where the large expanses of plate glass on the ground floor give the impression of a building that has had its legs chopped off. The large red-brick range in Sidney Street that contains Next and Marks and Spencer is a prime example, where it is as if two entirely different buildings have been slid one on top of the other. Another clear defect is the over-large size of the fascia boards and lettering. A sign does not have to be several feet tall to be seen and read, as witness street-name signs. But that does not stop big retail chains from shouting at people with their large and lurid boards. Sidney Street in particular has fallen victim to sign obesity, with the result that some of its retail units resemble pound shops in a depressed town.

*Careful highlighting of detail and simple, clear signage make for a distinguished shop front - Brian Jordan in Green Street.*

*Could this, by any remote chance, be the Phones4U store?*

*Clashing colours on Market Street.*

In many cases one sign is not considered sufficient. Phones4U at the corner of Petty Cury appears to be so terrified that shoppers will unheedingly pass them by that they have plastered huge signs on every available surface and have also affixed pendant signboards. In size, colour and excess the display is aggressive and crass. How many signs do they need? What happens at Phones4U sales conferences? Do they dispense with name badges and paint themselves orange from head to foot in order to proclaim their unique identity?

*One of the Victorian heads that adorn the façade of HK Fusion in St John's Street.*

Alas, too many shops are given the head-to-foot treatment. Instead of a painted signboard the whole ground floor is painted – brick, wood, the lot – often in strident colours that clash not only with the building above but also with neighbouring shop fronts. The particularly nasty row of competing colours in Market Street, pictured above, shows what the result can be. Architectural details are also painted over rather than being picked out, as in Karen Miller's all black frontage which runs up to the next storey. And a sad disregard for an especially striking building can be found at HK Fusion in St John's Street. Look up above the signage to see what you are missing, and what the shop has scant interest in.

75

*Differing approaches to signage on established buildings, in Trinity Street (left) and Bridge Street (right).*

Another building spoilt by insensitivity is the Arts and Crafts former bank just beyond Trinity Great Gate, now yet another designer clothes shop. The signs on the windows are discreet enough, but the company wants to attract attention from further down the street – despite occupying one of the most striking buildings in it – so a signboard has been crudely bolted on that overhangs and cuts across the arch of the doorway in a manner that could not be more irritatingly inappropriate. The sign recently had to be repaired, presumably having been hit by a passing lorry. Much more sensitive and comely is Patisserie Valerie on the corner of Bridge Street and Jesus Lane, with its neat lettering, clean colours and great respect for the building on this prominent corner site.

Choice of colour is a test of taste. Certain kinds of shops predictably pick red to stand out; Café Rouge in Bridge Street certainly lives up to its name. Unfortunately this tactic fails to work if your neighbours decide to do the same, as in Sidney Street where Rymans, Quicksilver, the Flight Centre and Santander all yell together. By contrast, Joules in Trinity Street has chosen downmarket custard yellow for a building that seems to invite more respectful treatment. This used to be the premises of antiquarian bookseller Deighton Bell, and was then clad in more distinguished livery.

If some shops are too lurid, a surprising number of others go to the opposite extreme. Perhaps Depression Grey and Suicide Black reflect (so to speak) the mood of society; certainly clothing has been mournfully muddy for far too long. Too many façades are in white, grey or black. Mud brown also makes its appearance, while others opt for exciting magnolia, that no-choice of the 1970s. Furthermore, the laziness of painting uniformly over a whole façade, irrespective of interesting details, extends to the entrance doors

*A variety of shop front colours in Trinity Street, ranging from mud brown and depression black, through custard yellow, to stark, uncompromising white.*

*'Toned-down' colour in visually sensitive Rose Crescent.*

which ought to stand out as a contrast. After all, no one camouflages the front door of his house. And where a business spreads to fill two retail units, one of the doors is usually blocked off, reducing the openness and variety of the street, an effect increased by the display of a greater area of the same colour.

Still, it could be a lot worse. The council planners very firmly told McDonalds that their full, gaudy signage was most definitely unwelcome in Rose Crescent, for which we may be extremely thankful. And there are a number of exemplary façades, some of the most satisfying being of varnished rather than painted wood. These harmonise better with the overall building, as can be seen at Arthur Shepherd or Ryder and Amies.

The latest draft of the Local Plan, published when the text for this book was almost complete, makes encouraging recommendations for more coherent and integrated street furniture and for improved shop signage ('signage should be subtle'). A visual pollution policy also suggests a reduction in street furniture to that which is absolutely necessary – though one has to ask who put it there in the first place. A Shop Front Design Guide already exists; how far the new policies will remain little more than words on a page is anyone's guess.

*A quiet and dignified shop front that still attracts the eye, in Trinity Street.*

## Open spaces

The centre is also made unpleasant by the use to which some buildings are put and by the use, or misuse, of open spaces. The growth of night clubs and mega-pubs has greatly increased the amount of drunken and violent behaviour, reducing the centre to a virtual no-go area in the late evening for anyone other than binge drinkers. A couple of decades ago it was possible to return from a late-night film at the Arts Cinema at 1 a.m. and cycle through deserted streets. Today, police vans move in on a Friday evening to deal with potential mayhem. In the daytime, pavements are colonised not only by cafés – presumably they pay rent to the council for commandeering this public space? – but also by buskers who use amplification that sends their noise into adjacent buildings, including college libraries.

*The rising popularity of Mediterranean-style al fresco dining has resulted in pedestrian areas becoming clogged with chairs and tables, as here on the corner of Market Street and Market Hill.*

Good buskers lend interest to the street scene, but many simply advertise the merits of ear plugs. It might be going too far to say that buskers should be auditioned before being granted a pitch, but a ban on amplified sound would be a kindness; we suffer enough unwanted music inside shops. And can anything be done about the sad groups of smokers huddled in chilly doorways? For non-smokers, the ban on smoking inside public buildings was one of the best pieces of legislation ever enacted. No longer did one have to wear 'drinking clothes' to visit a pub, or fan smoke away from one's food in a restaurant. But the unintended consequences are outdoor pockets of miasma through which others have to go, and a nasty detritus of cigarette ends on the pavement. Perhaps some of the institutions whose doorways are thus affected – the Arts Theatre being a notable example – could provide smoking rooms for their addicts and thereby remove a public nuisance.

# Locations marred, and places imperilled

Nicholas Pevsner, during his time as Slade Professor of Fine Art, wrote of his delight in Cambridge at 'being able to walk through a town for a whole mile without being hurt by the sight of a single building'. That was in 1952. You can still do so, provided you choose your route carefully. Since Pevsner's time there has even been a good deal of tidying up and improvement. Regrettably there has also been a good deal of architectural vandalism. Today, there is the threat of more vandalism to come.

## The market square

The market square retains something of its small country town feel, despite extensive rebuilding in the 20th century. The west side is attractively bounded by Great St Mary's Church, with views beyond to King's College, the University Schools and the Senate House. The east side is a jumble of styles, picturesque like King's Parade, and includes a fine 17th-century house with a shell hood above the first-floor balcony door. One might wish the former Victoria cinema, now Marks and Spencer, had not been built in that range. The north side contains the first Modernist building in Cambridge, designed in 1934 by Murray Easton as part of St Michael's Court, Caius College.

*Left: St Michael's Court, Cambridge's first Modern Movement building, on the market square.*

*Right: The jazzy modernity of Radcliffe Court elbows its way into Market Street.*

The main façade is not flat, as it seems from the front, but slightly curved, its Art Deco-inspired lines becoming more apparent as one walks along it. The junction with Rose Crescent is less satisfactory, and seen from the square, the building's glaring white uniformity looks out of place. Over to the right, in the northeast corner, Radcliffe Court (1964) – a zigzag piece of more recent modernity – also jars.

The square is overshadowed and heavily dominated by the Guildhall of 1938. John Steegman, in his book 'Cambridge' (Batsford 1940), writes persuasively of the building's dignity, good proportions and intelligent fenestration; but its dark brick, height and mass are all out of place here. It is quite different in scale from the guildhall it replaced, and while it is not much taller than the neighbouring buildings, it appears to overfill the whole side of the square. Such inflated size and overbearing aspect seem appropriate for a bureaucracy that requires ever more offices.

There have been ill-judged proposals to smarten up the square and to turn it into some imaginary continental piazza, all marble and tables with umbrellas and people drinking ouzo in the blazing sun. Pavements are already colonised by restaurants and cafés, particularly at the corners of the

*Modern and Victorian visions of civic grandeur side by side, with the former Central Library dwarfed by the 1930s Guildhall.*

*Facing Page*

*Top: The market square, an island of independent traders besieged by chain stores.*

*Bottom: The woeful 'memorial' to Snowy Farr - those familiar with him have a hard time recognising its purpose, and those who are not don't stand a chance.*

market square where pedestrian congestion is bad enough as it is. Anyone who thinks that a continental makeover is a good idea should look at Birmingham's Bull Ring, whose soul was destroyed in the 1960s by similar modernisation and the increase in market-stall rents that went with it.

A harbinger of potential Disneyfication can be seen in the ludicrous 'memorial' to Snowy Farr. It was an admirable idea to commemorate the eccentric who raised so much for charity, but a deplorable outcome that nothing better could be conceived than this pile of boiled sweets under a top hat.

The current market is living history, an extremely important survival of the kind of trading that has existed for hundreds of years. Even today it looks much the same as it did in 1860, as the photographs overleaf show. Shopping here is a very different experience from shopping in a modern mall. The market sells necessities – bread, cheese, fruit and vegetables – not designer handbags. It embodies a normality, an unpretentious authenticity and a cultural continuity that should be protected from ambitious, meddlesome designs and the greed of higher rents. This is the real Cambridge.

*These two photographs of Market Hill, taken from the same spot in 1860 and 2013, reveal a genuine historical continuity increasingly rare as Cambridge repositions itself to cater for wealthy visitors instead of residents.*

## Lion Yard and the Grand Arcade

In our climate, the covered market has much to recommend it. Oxford had one long ago. Cambridge put up a modern version in 1975, by which time the preferred terminology was 'shopping precinct' – more upmarket, so to speak. The construction of Lion Yard prior to the arrival of out-of-town retail parks in the 1980s prevented an exodus of shoppers from the centre. This in turn led to the building of the Grand Arcade adjacent to it thirty years later. Whether all this has been wholly desirable is another matter.

It was characteristic of the time that for Lion Yard a huge area was flattened, including one whole side of Petty Cury and the remains of the 17th-century Falcon Inn and Red Lion Hotel. Such large-scale construction was costly. In consequence, rents were pitched high and the range of 'useful' shops soon contracted, until for some people the library was the only reason for going there. The building of the Grand Arcade at least ensured that John Lewis, Cambridge's last major department store, remained in the city centre. But otherwise it just meant the arrival of more designer-clothing and 'lifestyle' shops belonging to mega-companies big enough to swallow the eye-watering rents.

*The entrance to Lion Yard in Petty Cury.*

*The Grand Arcade, looking north towards Lion Yard.*

This is a pity. The Grand Arcade provides a handsome space with attractive natural top lighting. The materials are of good quality and blend together well, while the galleries above create a sense of theatre. It is a place that invites you to linger. But for what? At times it feels like an expensive white elephant, with most of its shops selling exorbitantly priced luxury and lifestyle goods of little interest to the average person. But perhaps this is merely the view of a male who doesn't 'do shopping'.

A number of questions niggle. When Lion Yard was refurbished in 1999, why was the central handrail removed from the ramp leading up from Petty Cury? This must present problems for the elderly, or those unsteady on their feet, despite the non-slip surface that was laid down at the same time. And what became of the large wooden red lion that formerly stood outside the library, and the pillar commemorating the architects, civil engineers and council officials responsible for the original Lion Yard development? Do we perhaps detect the hand of the corporate re-branders who loathe history? And why are portcullises deemed necessary at the Lion Yard entrances? Why are automatic doors being mooted for the Grand Arcade? They are unlikely to exclude 'draughts' since they will hardly ever be shut, given the incessant pedestrian traffic. And what is wrong with fresh air anyway?

*Lion Yard's east gate with portcullis raised.*

*Above and right: Characterless regiment-
ation and historically evolved variety face
each other the entire length of Petty Cury.*

## Petty Cury

Petty Cury was, of course, wrecked by the construction of Lion Yard. The street is undoubtedly improved by the removal of all wheeled traffic and the creation of further and covered pedestrian space under the loggia of the new buildings, but visually it is appalling. The monotonous uniformity of the Lion Yard façade and its hanging shop signs contrasts unfavourably with the varied styles and rooflines of the old side. Its regimented design does not curve enticingly with the street but is composed of two long straight lines angled slightly away from a pointless, ugly arched entrance too tall to be properly seen in the narrow thoroughfare (see photo on p. 83). The white-painted concrete pillars are brash and out of context. There is no sensible roofline, no pediment, just a sense of incompleteness and temporariness, like a stage flat. At each end, the materials fail to blend in with either St Andrew's Church or the Guildhall corner of the market square. The view from the corner of Sidney Street and Market Street towards St Andrew's presents a particularly disagreeable sense of incongruity, the white posts drawing the eye like ill-judged 'bling' or a startling neck-tie. Turn to the right and look up Market Street, where Holy Trinity Church and E.S. Prior's Henry Martyn Hall in quite different materials create a much more inviting prospect.

*Blundell Court, Sidney Sussex - a building so tall it has to disguise its top storey with lighter materials.*

## King Street

The wholesale redevelopment of entire streets never seems to work well, and King Street, like Petty Cury, has also had its pleasing variety of historical accretions obliterated by uniform monotony. Some of the replacement buildings, such as Manor Place (see photo opposite), are neat enough, yet they do not add up to a satisfactory street. But the real damage has been done by the colleges; two back onto King Street, and their newer additions have had a disastrous effect upon it. In 1967, Sidney Sussex built Blundell Court, a tall block rising above the wall on the corner of Hobson Street with barely a shred of cover, as would be decent, from trees, while on King Street's south side, Christ's College disfigured the location in 1970 with their New Court, designed by Denys Lasdun, the architect who had proposed 200-foot towers for the New Museums Site. (There must have been some relief in Cambridge when he retired soon after.) The front, viewed from inside the college, was striking, but its rear end stuck out horribly into King Street like the back of a football terrace. It was some time before Christ's could either afford or recognise the need for amelioration and gave the unsightly horror a proper face to the street. There is a more

*The former football terrace of New Court, Christ's College, used to bare its Brutalist backside to the street. Nowadays it is modestly clad in brick-faced retail units.*

*The long façade of Manor Place, King Street.*

pleasing development at the east end of the street. Epworth Court, a group of retirement flats on the south side, displays an attractive roof line and interesting angles when seen from the west.

*Epworth Court, a more successful addition to King Street's mix of old and new architecture.*

## Drummer Street

This congested bus station site is a shadow of what it might have been if earlier proposals had been carried through. In his 1950 report, town planner William Holford had suggested a much bigger station, taking up the site now occupied by the Christ's Lane development (formerly Bradwell's Court). It would also have meant the sacrifice of a larger portion of Christ's Pieces, not to mention building an insane 'Spine Relief Road' which would have bisected the Pieces and effectively destroyed them (see Chapter 11). The idea of locating a bus station between two colleges could scarcely be more hostile to the notion of cloistered calm. The present design makes at least some attempt at congruity with Christ's Pieces by masquerading as a giant greenhouse; from a distance one might suppose there were botanic specimens to be seen there.

Re-opening Christ's Lane improved pedestrian access to the city centre, but Emmanuel Street remains as congested as ever; heaven help anyone who wants to cross it to catch a bus there at busy times. Relocating to the railway station area has been suggested, but that too has its problems, not least that there is no money in it for developers.

*Drummer Street bus station, with its echoes of Joseph Paxton's Crystal Palace, thoughtfully hides its utilitarian purpose from viewers on Christ's Pieces.*

*The same structure, viewed from Drummer Street, is elegantly functional.*

*Emmanuel Street, lined end-to-end with bus shelters and menaced by the towering tsunami of the Grand Arcade.*

## Corn Exchange Street

This is a disaster, a descent into hell. It is the ugliest street in the centre of
Cambridge and has been made so entirely within living memory. We can
see this from earlier pictures. A photograph of 1865 shows an extremely
narrow, shabby cobbled lane of two- and three-storey buildings with room
for only one footpath. It was then known as Slaughter House Lane and if
nothing else it looks quaint. On one side is a coal merchant's and a stretch
of blank wall, but on the other are houses and shops, doors and windows,
and therefore some openness to the street. Today the frontages are almost
entirely closed. There is nothing to see or do. The redevelopments of the
1960s and subsequently have made nothing of this thoroughfare. It is
merely a conduit for pouring vehicles into the Grand Arcade car park.
Although wider than it was in 1865, it still has only one tiny footpath at
street level; to negotiate Corn Exchange Street safely, the luckless
pedestrian must use a raised walkway inside the car park on the east side.

*'Someone had
blundered...'*

*The southern entrance to
Corn Exchange Street.*

*Slaughter House Lane in 1865.*

But it is not just the problems at ground level that we notice. The street dips down and then rises, bringing the upper levels more obviously into view. Though people rarely look up, the nightmare landscape here is unmissable, the view architecturally incoherent. The photograph on the facing page shows the southern entrance to the street. Is this Sheffield? Some sort of awful mistake? ('Someone had blundered ... Blank walls to the right of them, Brutalism to the left of them, Motor cars ahead of them... Into the mouth of Hell drove the six hundred', etc. etc.)

The Brutalism to the left of them, reminiscent of London's South Bank, is the Arup Building (1971). This houses the University Department of Materials Science and Metallurgy, and ironically is fashioned from some of the nastiest materials known to builders. Here is a University backside exposed, with buildings that have no sensible relationship to the street at all; perhaps respectful treatment was thought unnecessary when looking across at a multistorey car park.

*Fortunately one of the best kept secrets on Cambridge's tourist trail - a gobsmacking view of the Arup Building on the New Museums Site from the Grand Arcade car park.*

The original proposals for the New Museums Site, drawn up in 1961, included two tower blocks over 200 feet high and one of 150 feet. Balloons were put up to indicate their height; unsurprisingly they were visible from just about everywhere. The effect on the famous view of King's from the Backs would have been so crassly offensive as to beggar belief that any sane person could have dreamt it up, except as a joke. Two more versions were submitted before the ludicrous scheme was finally dropped. It was a narrow escape. But it was not the only time the university or the colleges have shown contempt for the town in this way.

The southern entrance to the street says something about the architectural standards of two different periods and institutions. On the left is the Humphrey Museum and on the right the Cambridge City Hotel (previously the Crowne Plaza, and once upon a time the Holiday Inn). The former is sober, worthy and dull, like many Edwardian civic buildings, but at least it turns the corner gracefully. The hotel does not. This foolish building was much derided when it went up in 1991, and the Royal Fine Art Commission described it as 'sadly illiterate'. If scorn could flatten a structure, it would have been a heap of rubble long ago.

*Guildhall Place - a good attempt at making use of an awkward space.*

*Facing page*

*Top: Part of the unremittingly grim façade of the Department of Metallurgy and Materials Science.*

*Bottom: The Disney Classicism of the Cambridge City Hotel, aka Barbie's Mansion.*

For some reason the developers thought it appropriate to avoid frightening people with a genuinely contemporary style, and instead went for a selection of simple pseudo-classical motifs to decorate what might almost be stage scenery. Perhaps the nearby classical columns of Emmanuel College inspired them to this folly. But it is not even pastiche. The windows stare blankly with no glazing bars and there are no cornices above the wings on either side of the pediment. There is a hopelessly inappropriate metal and glass entrance canopy tacked onto the front, resembling fragments of the Crystal Palace. The new John Lewis building further along Downing Street is properly of its time and far better.

The northern end of the street opposite the Corn Exchange attempts to create some sort of coherence out of a jumble of ill-assorted buildings, with a little square, *plads* or piazza, which to continentals means not simply an open space but an inviting space, comfortably enclosed. There is a raised terrace overlooking the area, some steps, and a half-encircling wall with benches in a sunny corner, but it is an apology for a piazza, nothing that says this is a place to arrive at, or to stop in. There are too many visible exits, while the benches have no backs and no worthwhile view. Above everything looms the wall of the Grand Arcade, making the umbrellas on the terrace look like the tents of besiegers at the foot of a huge fortress. But at least an effort has been made, as it has with part of the ground floor of the car park. This could easily have been a closed frontage, but where there would otherwise have been a blank wall, there is a secure cycle parking facility and a cycle shop. Useful shops are now scarce in the city centre; we should be grateful that somebody thought to open this one in what would appear to be an unlikely spot for a retail outlet.

*The entrance to the Grand Arcade cycle park and shop windows of Station Cycles in Corn Exchange Street.*

The city centre is a preservation area teeming with listed buildings, but that has not prevented the intrusion of undesirable features. The new Local Plan suggests that the council is belatedly waking up to the threat of out-of-scale buildings and the disfigurements of shop front design, street furniture and paving. The question is whether or not it can actually bring its policies into effect. The probable redevelopment of the Mill Lane area will be a revealing test.

A further danger may come from too much meddling and too many conscious attempts to change the character of the centre, as for instance in repeated proposals to smarten up the market square. The present stalls appear little different from those of 1860, and there is much to be said for retaining their unpretentious look, and maintaining a genuine historic continuity which is every bit as valid as that of old college buildings. Spare us from clutter by all means, but spare us also from metropolitan slickness and banal copycat buildings. This is Cambridge, not Dubai.

# 4

# New university and college buildings

*This chapter does not cover all the modern additions to Cambridge's university and college buildings, but concentrates instead on those that are most obviously visible to the general public; thus, for example, the jumbled mediocrity of the interior of Downing Museums and Laboratories Site is not discussed, nor are the most recent developments in West Cambridge, except as they impinge on Madingley Road or the Coton footpath.*

## The university

During the 1960s much new building went up for both the university and the colleges. There was a particular need to provide better accommodation for the subject faculties, not only for teaching but also for social purposes. Previously, members of the same faculty but from different colleges might rarely cross paths. University teachers who were not college Fellows were even more isolated, and postgraduate students – who belonged neither to the Senior Combination Room nor to the JCR – were growing in number; a social centre for them was badly needed.

*The spirit of the 1960s - early buildings on the Sidgwick site.*

To tackle the first problem, work on the Sidgwick Site began in 1958. The aim was to build a modern campus of Arts Faculty buildings west of the river to a master plan devised in 1952 by Sir Hugh Casson. However, details of the plan came in for considerable criticism, such that the original scheme was not carried through and other architects were brought in. The results were disappointing.

Hugh Plommer, dedicated to classical architecture, found fault with every building on the site and published his speeches to the University Senate in a booklet 'The Line of Duty' (1982). 'Nothing can be more banal than the results of attempted modernity and of singularity at all costs', he wrote, and he complained of 'a weary succession of worthless designs'.

It is hard not to agree with many of his strictures against the Modernism of the 1960s. One of the most reviled buildings on the site is James Stirling's History Faculty. Its appearance has divided opinion, many disliking its industrial/commercial look, the strong, dark red brick and the extensive greenhouse glazing; but more significantly it fails to do what all buildings are fundamentally meant to do – keep out the weather. Under leaky glass, readers in the library are fried in summer and frozen in winter, while the open tiers of seating echo loudly and fail to create the calm such a place should possess. It shows the dangers of employing an architect known for startling, bold gestures, something our city council seems to be worryingly and misguidedly keen on at present.

*The unfocussed entrance to the Sidgwick site, with naked car parking.*

*The long, dull shed of the Classics Faculty, Sidgwick Avenue.*

*The elegant, S-shaped Stephen Hawking Building, West Road.*

Stirling's design was the architectural equivalent of Punk Rock or Brit Art, deliberately setting out to shock, and the result was a predictable, posturing stunt. He later said he did it 'to fuck Casson'. What a contrast to the quiet sensitivity of Erik Sørensen's Crystallographic Data Centre building in Union Road (see p. 102), a structure obviously contemporary yet without 'in your face' gimmicks.

The approach to the site from Sidgwick Avenue is not encouraging. Coming from the Backs one is greeted by a windowless wall of brown brick rising above the older red brick wall of a long-demolished house. It could be something on a business park: it turns out to be the Classics Faculty. The site's main entrance is awful, a muddle of car parking, signs, bollards and buildings set in no coherent relation to one another. Amongst these scattered freestanding structures is a lecture block on stilts, the spaces beneath looking chilly and draughty. Several of the new universities of the 1960s did better than this in creating modern campuses.

The West Road side of the site is undergoing further development with designs that are already clichés. Peach-coloured cladding on the English Faculty recalls the prefabricated CLASP buildings of the 1960s. It has slats over ground floor windows that face the sunless north, but they are currently fashionable and so must be included. The Stephen Hawking Building, stone faced, is the one structure of real quality on this frontage.

*The English Faculty, a treasury of current architectural clichés, bleakly faces West Road.*

A meeting place for graduate students was built in 1963 by Mill Lane, overlooking the Mill Pool. The Cambridge University Centre or 'Grad Pad' is a perfect example of a building in the wrong place. The riverside deserves better than this brutal concrete box with bolt-on stone cladding. Both its materials and its bulk are offensive in this location. It has been described as a multistorey car park with windows, but there is also the feeling of a fortress about it. The ground floor is 'closed', that is, the pedestrian encounters a blank brick wall with windows above head height. Significantly, this slopes outwards like the base or talus of a castle. Looking up, one sees a roof with an overhanging parapet reminiscent of machicolation, so that one half expects boiling oil to come pouring down. The windows that are so pleasant to look out of are reflective, and therefore darkened to passers-by, and the whole impression is of a self-contained world of privilege, jealously guarding its advantages and presenting a hostile front to *hoi polloi*.

*Old Vernacular meets New Brutalism in Granta Place. Which would you rather have a pint in?*

*Facing page*

*Top: A peasant's eye view of the Grad Pad's façade and parapet.*

*Bottom: A defensive talus and mirrored windows contribute to the building's forbidding aspect.*

Another fortress-like edifice is the Castle Building, pictured overleaf, which forms the rear entrance to the Judge Institute of Management Studies in Tennis Court Road. Standing in the back yard of old Addenbrooke's, its startling playfulness can be experienced without any sense of an older landscape being violated. It is not a restful building and reminds one of a heavily tattooed and metal-pierced individual, but its exuberant display is more rewarding than the raw utilitarianism of the Graduate Centre. The institute's main building, facing Trumpington Street, is an imaginative transformation of the former hospital and, while not to everyone's taste, it succeeds in combining panache with sensitivity to the original features of the building. The result is eye-catching, intriguing and stimulating; it has lifted and

brightened the façade of the former hospital while preserving a piece of old Cambridge that could so easily have gone to destruction.

Round the corner in Lensfield Road, the Scott Polar Institute has been sensitively extended with a new library, a far better performance than the earlier extension at the rear. The adjacent Chemistry Laboratories, completed in 1960 and more recently given a face-lift on the Union Road side, are dreadfully out of scale with their surroundings. Although stylistically they hark back to 1930s Modernism they are all too typical of their time, when respect for anything older was abandoned in the rush to modernity and vain posturing. They are reminiscent of the mood often referred to in Harold Wilson's words – the 'white heat' of the scientific revolution – which certainly burnt a good deal that lay in its path.

*The Judge Institute's Castle Building - more bouncy castle than grim fortress.*

*The Isaac Newton building.*

*The largest of the Isaac Newton Institute's 'pagodas' - the Märit and Hans Rausing Pavilion.*

Other university buildings, mostly good, have appeared in the Grange Road area in recent years. The Needham Research Institute with its Chinese references sits well in its garden in Sylvester Road. A little distance away in Clarkson Road, the Isaac Newton Institute for Mathematical Sciences is striking and harmoniously composed. Eight pagoda-like pavilions display an inventiveness of surface forms tempered by the use of simple, monochrome materials. They are perfectly placed in relation to one another, the spaces between them forming part of a satisfying compositional rhythm. The Isaac Newton building, which stands at the entrance to the site, is not so accomplished, lacking as it does the originality and panache of the 'pagodas'. A somewhat incompatible combination of dormers and a lantern disturbs the harmony of the roof, while lower down, the gaping entrance of glass and white wood is stylistically incongruous, reminiscent of a 1960s community centre. But overall, the institute's buildings are a welcome change from the dreary glass and concrete boxes that have predominated for so long.

One of the finest new buildings of all is the Crystallographic Data Centre (1992) in Union Road. At first sight, and at a little distance, one is aware of a large expanse of red brick, superficially rather dull. But something about it says 'quality'. On closer inspection one notices the characteristic narrow bricks of Denmark and the equally characteristic Danish skill in handling them. And Danish it is. The bricks were made in Flensburg, close to the Danish border, and the architect was Erik Christian Sørensen, who died in August 2011. The crisp, clean use of brick, the nicely judged details and the well-mannered unobtrusiveness all display the best of modern Danish architecture. The building does not need to scream at us to impress. On a sunny day, the effects of light and shade on this carefully calculated façade are serene and satisfying. It is beautifully adapted to its awkward site and shows what can be done with care and good-quality materials. It is a thousand pities that a traffic sign has been placed against the building when it could just as easily have been to one side – a typical council Pooter-man act of utter gormlessness. The façade might as well have been sprayed with graffiti; such fine architecture should be treated with more consideration.

One needs to keep an eye on Mill Lane and its surroundings. In 2009, the university revealed plans to demolish a large part of this area – including the lecture theatres – to make way for shops, offices, restaurants, flats and a 70-room hotel. High-density development is being aimed at, which prompted Councillor Colin Rosenthiel to comment, 'I trust we won't have any more proposals for out-of-scale building here, as on some other central sites in schemes put forward by other developers'. Well, there's no harm in hoping.

The university's West Cambridge site has already been mentioned in the description of the Madingley Road approach (Chapter 2). Development has reached the Coton footpath to the south and is opening up what was until fairly recently a rural path. Much of it is screened, in the summer at least, by tall hawthorn hedges, but side access paths reveal substantial building all the way to the M11. University science requires ever larger and more numerous buildings in order to stay in the front rank, and 'dynamic' persons will say that if you are standing still you are actually going backwards. One does wonder where or when it will all end – when the whole country is built up from coast to coast, perhaps?

*Facing Page*

*The skilfully patterned and punctuated brick façade of Sørensen's Crystallographic Data Centre.*

Several 'cutting edge' buildings have recently gone up on the West Cambridge site, though the Cavendish Laboratory, which can be seen from the Coton footpath, is not one of them; it is dull, boxy, functional, even industrial, and would not look out of place beside the dreariest railway siding. Next to it is the newer, 'hi there, I'm really modern' Hauser Forum building. This grey and white, part-chequered, part-stripy box, with slats across the windows and a slatted canopy of no obvious utility, fulfils many of the requirements for contemporary cliché. A terrace of bilious lime-coloured chairs and tables looks out over the fields, and one hopes that trees will quickly grow up to hide as much of it as possible.

*Residential blocks on the West Cambridge Site.*

Beyond it stand residential blocks in grey and blue. They are neat but drab, and nothing dates faster than colour. At least they rise no higher than the surrounding tree tops. Further on, the new Department of Materials Science and Metallurgy rises high above the bushes along the path, but tree planting has also gone in and should in time ameliorate the effect. The landscaping here looks promising, with a fine lake between the building and the path. Turning to come back into town, one is reminded that one of Cambridge's least lovely towers stands directly along its sightline – the University Library, with its hints of Mordor.

*The Hauser Forum viewed from the Coton footpath.*

*The Cavendish Laboratory.*

*The new Department of Materials Science and Metallurgy.*

# The colleges

Leaving aside the commercial properties they might develop, colleges build for themselves. They have, broadly speaking, money, time and – or so one hopes – taste. Quick profits are not necessarily their chief concern. A new library is a scholastic proposition rather than one of business, and every detail matters in a building designed for long and comfortable use. Most importantly, the people commissioning the building are the people who will be using it.

There have been some excellent results in consequence. Recent new libraries have been particularly successful, as at Jesus College and St John's. The most important, because the most conspicuously sited, is the Jerwood Library of Trinity Hall. Completed in 1998, it immediately looked right. It was not quite as if it had always been there – it is clearly a modern building – but as if it was always meant to be there. Its position and design command attention, yet its materials, in harmony with the adjacent older buildings, and the small scale of its component parts, prevent it from being unduly dominant. Its footprint is tiny, and the architects did a fine job in providing the required accommodation within its boundaries. It is the best addition to the landscape of the Backs in modern times.

*Disaster and triumph. Queens' College's contribution to the landscape of the Backs (left), contrasted with that of Trinity Hall (facing page).*

In contrast there have been some notorious catastrophes. The Cripps Court and Lyon Court development at Queens' is shocking in every way. in materials, in design, in location. It occupies one of the most sensitive sites in the whole of Cambridge and is of huge proportions. The immediate built environment is of brick, yet into this subdued setting the college has introduced near-Brutalist buildings of glaring white concrete that have no reference to their surroundings. It is as if the Fellows had been determined to show that they were not hidebound by tradition and could be bold, new and up-to-date. It would have been much the same had they decided to see how best they could ruin their part of the Backs.

*This and facing page:*

*Trinity Hall triumphs again - vernacular references and fine materials at Wychfield.*

To the west of the Backs stand various outliers of the colleges, constructed to meet the need for further accommodation. One of the most impressive is the newest addition to Trinity Hall's Wychfield site on Storey's Way, commissioned from RH Partnership Architects and completed in 2007. At first sight this might be a grouping of malting houses or barn conversions. What immediately strikes one about these buildings, aside from their superb proportions, is their use of vernacular materials, which shows perfect sensitivity to their location: wood, brick and tile are particularly apt in a residential road that contains several houses by Baillie Scott. Even the neat iron gates are softened by wooden cladding to the pillars. The variegated brick is especially attractive and the blankness of the gable walls facing the road is alleviated by tile hanging, something of an aesthetic stunt but a good one. The development is beautifully laid out, aligned away from the road with respect for the neighbouring houses, and containing peaceful formal gardens between the ranges with trees at the end of each vista. Even something as basic and functional as a bike shed is thoughtfully treated, its roof sloping to the beech hedge in a way that creates a harmonious composition. The ranges appear at first to be identical, but in fact possess welcome variations. Only in the westernmost group is there a discordant note, where between two short ranges a third projects at 90 degrees, looking like an old-fashioned television clad in wood. But overall this is a superb development, eye-catching in the right way. It justly received the David Unwin Award for architecture in 2011.

A little further along Storey's Way, Fitzwilliam – a college whose original architecture is astonishingly bleak – has built a neat and handsome range, with the college arms in stone identifying its new entrance. The brick is of a pleasing colour (unlike the original buildings) and the fenestration is excellent, but the glass lantern is a slightly irritating modern cliché. Resembling a fish tank and providing only moderate illumination, it nonetheless identifies the entrance and gives balance to the essentially horizontal composition. The hedge is a nice touch; copper and green beech alternate to create a geometry echoing that of the windows behind it.

In Grange Road, other modern developments have been generally suc-cessful. Lined with red-brick houses and colleges – notably Newnham and Selwyn – it was mercifully spared unsympathetic modern glass and concrete when Robinson College was built in 1980. Though concrete-framed, Robinson's buildings are clad in a red brick that is already quietly retiring behind increasingly well-established trees and shrubs. They are

*Neat composition at Fitzwilliam echoed in the planting of the hedge. Shame about the fish tank, though.*

carefully arranged along the perimeter of the grounds, thereby preserving much of the garden and mature trees that pre-dated them. (How many speculative developers would have resisted the temptation to start with a completely razed plot?)

The high-quality brickwork still looks fresh and new after thirty years. The entrance is a modern take on the college gate tower, and also resembles a castle with its tower and entrance ramp (as if over a moat). In 1983 it justly gained an award for Architectural Excellence from the Royal Institute of British Architecture. Two niggling details of street furniture spoil the approach, however. Yellow traffic-calming bollards stand just outside, and a lamp-post is carelessly placed right in front of the college's slate name sign. Perhaps it is simply an unhappy accident of electrical circuitry or spacing, but only a few feet to the left and the lamp would be far more harmoniously placed. A small matter, maybe, but so is bird lime on a window. We do not want it there.

*Convincing castle references at Robinson College.*

Further along, Selwyn has added a good, clean red-brick neo-Georgian range which fits in well with the old red house on the site. Opposite this, on the corner of Cranmer Road, the earlier Cripps Court seems incongruous. Its flint-faced walls and white-painted chevron rooflines bring to mind a trendy 1960s church. The use of flint is mystifying.

Nearby Clare Hall is not entirely successful, though some think otherwise. On the Michael Stoker Building (1988) one notices the 'stunts' first – the metal railings and stairways and the odd, boxed-in staircase stuck onto the side. The zigzag structure brings the word 'jazzy' to mind and the sharp angles quite ignore and spoil the setting of the retiring Edwardian house beyond. The development is decently proportioned, rather boxy but low, in places resembling council flats rather than college residences, although this was deliberate. A very visible subterranean car and bike park add to the municipal effect.

*Selwyn's Cripps Court - 1960s trendiness in Victorian and Edwardian Grange Road.*

In the centre of town the colleges have not made much of King Street, as described in the previous chapter. Sidney Sussex, understandably cramped for space, has two looming residential blocks and no screening to mitigate their baleful effect on the corner of Hobson Street. Further along, Christ's committed the visual atrocity of the Lasdun building which they later had the grace to clothe more decently (see p. 87). The effect, while not wholly satisfactory, is better than it was.

On a happier note, in 1997 Pembroke College added Foundress Court, a very handsome set of buildings by Eric Parry fronting Tennis Court Road. True, it has the now ubiquitous lantern (there is no escaping contemporary clichés entirely) but the quality of materials and finish make an immediately favourable impression. The neat cubes of freestanding Bath stone sit well with one another and the street. Parry took care that the buildings related just as effectively to the street as to the college grounds – how different from Lasdun at Christ's. A particularly nice touch is the sundial cut into the stone of the third-storey wall; it relieves what would otherwise have been a large blank. The college wanted buildings that avoided untested technology and would have a long life expectancy, but they also asked for buildings of their time that might claim to be the best new college buildings in Cambridge; it may fairly be argued that Parry succeeded with this brief.

*Foundress Court at Pembroke, designed to enhance public as well as private space.*

*Foundress Court's sundial - only visible from the street, and thus a generous gesture by the architect and the college.*

College building in the last two decades has been generally well considered, with sensitivity to constricted sites and existing buildings. Where the university has a free hand, however, on the West Cambridge site, there is every likelihood that such restraint will not be shown. A virgin site, well away from the old centre, allows scope for exciting new architecture. It also removes the conditions that might prevent mere 'sensation-seeking stunts'. Time will tell which it is to be.

# 5

# Sturton Town and Romsey Town

At first sight this might seem to be an area worth demolishing entirely. Sixty years ago the Holford Report described the Gwydir Street zone as composed of 'third class housing'. In 1964 the authors of 'Cambridge New Architecture' described Romsey as 'a twilight area almost more drab than the close, intimate slum. Sooner or later it will need comprehensive redevelopment'. Thirty years ago when I was house hunting, my first impression of Romsey Town was, 'Blimey! Coronation Street!' Cycling up the long Mill Road, and seeing dead straight rows of Victorian terraced houses leading off to left and right, I couldn't imagine living there. In fact I did, for nineteen years, though luckily not in one of the more monotonous streets. For there were unexpected pleasant havens, and also, after a time, the place acquired agreeable memories and associations. Even so, I was glad when I eventually moved to a modern and better-designed house.

These Mill Road houses were speculative, not to say rudimentary, developments. Below the floorboards of my own terrace house lay the bare earth and what seemed sketchy foundations. In the loft, the party walls had next to no mortar between the bricks, and what there was flowed over like melted icing.

*Catharine Street.*

**115**

Between my house and my neighbour's there was a narrow V-shaped gap running from the top where, at some point, his house had subsided away from mine. It had been filled with mortar. One day early on, I was painting the ground-floor front window. An elderly couple passed, and I heard the man say to his wife, 'I thought they were demolishing these houses'. This was hardly encouraging, but I understood his view.

The area was then, in the 1980s, in the process of being gentrified. The interiors of these homes are now often very smart and command prices more preposterous than one would have thought possible for a two-up two-down Victorian railway worker's cottage – almost half a million pounds in Gwydir Street (Holford's 'third class housing'). Yet they remain very modest and ugly, with little or no front gardens and therefore little protection from street noise. And outside, parked vehicles crowd the narrow streets and pavements bumper-to-bumper, creating their own visual pollution. If you designed your own home – a modest, unostentatious building to meet normal requirements – a Mill Road house is unlikely to be what you would come up with, nor would you want it to be in a long street of identical dwellings with the ground floor windows half obliterated by rows of cloned cars.

*A forest of chimneys rises above Mill Road railway bridge, the meeting point of Romsey Town and Sturton Town.*

However, we have the Mill Road area at present and there seems little likelihood of its immediate demolition. Moreover, there is no guarantee that redevelopment would be an improvement; looking at Winstanley Court in Cromwell Road or the Stalinist flats of Rustat Avenue one is not optimistic. Furthermore, people actually like living in Romsey and Sturton Town. There is some sense of community, there is an annual street carnival and a winter fair, and residents, anxious to preserve the atmosphere, are protective of the small, independent shops. Romsey has recently become a conservation area.

*At Mill Road railway bridge, where unexpectedly leafy views delight the eye in densely-built Victorian Cambridge.*

Other favourable features came to my attention when, after spending an afternoon exploring the ghastly area by the station, I decided to return home via Mill Road. Reaching the railway bridge, I was struck by how pleasant and comfortable everything seemed by comparison with the place I had just left. The buildings were as ugly as ever, but two things stood out. Firstly, the road was on a human scale, with almost nothing over two storeys high. The effect on me was physical and immediate. I felt better instantly; I was in a place where humans belonged, unlike the windswept canyons of the Belvedere with its exterminating Dalek. Secondly, there were trees – more than I had really noticed before. As I stood on the bridge of this old workers' quarter I took in a green and leafy view in both directions. Looking across to Hills Road bridge I saw by contrast the nightmare landscape of the Rustat Avenue apartment blocks, the Marque, the Travelodge and the Belvedere, all buildings of recent construction. It was a relief to turn aside and look down Mill Road, with its punctuation of little rows of trees all the way down to Brookfields.

Apart from the trees, Mill Road has some unusually interesting and even attractive buildings. In such a busy street it is easy to overlook the details, but they are worth noticing. Without attempting an exhaustive list, attention may be drawn to the more striking examples. Between Brookfields and the Broadway, three in particular stand out as skilfully conceived.

*The south façade of Brookfields Hospital, viewed from Mill Road.*

Firstly, Brookfields Hospital, built in 1884. Under overcast skies this can seem gaunt and grim, but on a sunny day – particularly an autumn day of clear light – its best features stand out sharply. Buildings are like paintings; it is possible to go beyond a first impression to 'read' the details. What do we see of the hospital? Firstly there is a good deal of blank yellow brick, and the three ground-floor windows are high up and small. This is practical – it is a hospital and so it sensibly turns sideways from the noisy street, which would also have been dusty before the arrival of tarmac.

Then perhaps we notice three terracotta lines – string courses – drawn across the façade. They serve the practical purpose of channelling rain water away from the brick, but their colour also adds variety to the otherwise monotonous wall. The same use of colour applies to the window arches which, rather than being lazily horizontal, are curved to vary the lines on the façade. Turning to the windows themselves, we see that those on the first

*Civic pride in terracotta - the Cambridge Borough coat of arms.*

floor are not uniform. The central window forms a T shape, creating a balance and symmetry. To the right, where there are no windows, the blank wall is relieved by a kind of pilaster-cum-chimney stack, and a further element of interest is introduced by vertical red-brick lines running up to its top. But what especially draws the eye is the terracotta panel bearing the borough (now city) coat of arms, framed by Ionic scrolls and capped by a pediment. The close-up photograph, above, shows the detail, still sharp after a century. How many modern buildings bother to do anything like that? The panel is high up and can easily be missed, which reminds us of how important it is to look up at buildings.

*Brookfields Hospital's south and west façades (left), and detailing on a chimney stack (right).*

*Simplicity and good proportions displayed by Romsey Mill.*

The second building of note is Romsey Mill, facing Coleridge Road. This former Wesleyan Methodist Chapel (1906) is another pale yellow brick building with red brick details. At first sight it is plain and does not draw attention to itself. Though large, it is not heavy or overbearing – its bulk minimised by careful proportioning and simplicity of treatment – and it faces the corner well. Sadly it is disfigured by three signs in unsympathetic colours, and three where one ought to do. The white door is too bland and shows no regard for the colour of the brick, and one might also quibble about the ugly maroon paint of the blocked windows. The tree directly in front of it is a mistake; this would have been better placed further down the road. Removal of these small blemishes would do justice to a quietly impressive building.

*Garish modern signage mars Romsey Mill's façade.*

The third is the recently refurbished St Philip's Church of 1889. Like Brookfields Hospital, it is thoughtfully composed and repays a closer look. Prior to its renovation the immediate impression was probably dominated by an unfortunate modern entrance porch, doubtless a convenient feature and one which made an attempt to blend in. It was simple and neat, with the roof ridges radiating from the base of the central lancet window to touch visually the outer edges of the façade. But the bright red porch below was too heavy and boxy, set against the slender lancet windows and the steep gable; perhaps a less strident colour for the woodwork would have helped. The new porch is more in keeping. It is of brick, matching both the material and style of the original building. The contemporary-style additions are reasonably discreet with their grey-green window frames but, neat as they are, the café to the left and the infill to the right both distract attention from the old façade. It is also a pity to see the original south door bricked up and an excessive amount of brash, corporate-style signage. Nonetheless, an old building has been revitalised to meet modern needs and this has been done with some respect.

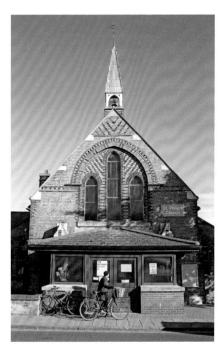 

*St Philip's Church, Mill Road, in 2010 (left), and following alteration in 2012 (right).*

The delicacy of the original conception is apparent once we raise our eyes above ground level. The eye is quickly taken up to the little bell tower and spire of well-judged height that carry on the line of the central lancet window. *En route* one is aware of the detailed patterning of red brick against the yellow-grey façade. On a dull day this can easily be missed but on a day of clear cold October air, such as when the photographs on this page were taken, the detail is sharply lit. Such bricklaying requires extra care to get the pattern right, and again one wonders how much comparable trouble is taken with modern buildings. Similar care has been taken over the steeple, which is decorated with little hooks, like crockets on a pinnacle, and with patterned edges to its layers of lead. The thin cross at its summit lies within a circle to prevent it seeming too slight and unnoticeable.

*Below. The original sign on St Philip's Church (left), and the corporate-style branding that replaced it (right).*

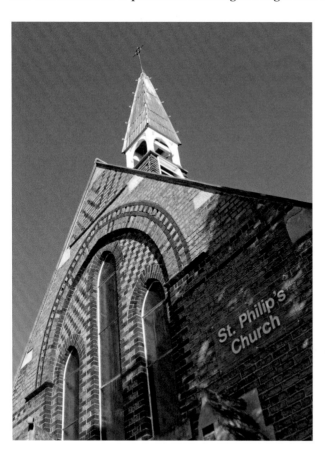

*Facing page top: Intricate detailing in brick on the west window of St Philip's Church.*

*Right and below: The Baptist Church Centre, Stockwell Street - an example of sensitive infill.*

At the other end of the Broadway stands Mill Road Baptist Church. The Mill Road façade hardly warrants a second glance but behind it, round the corner into Stockwell Street, a very good piece of modern infilling has taken place in the form of the Baptist Church Centre. This fits in harmoniously between the church and the terrace of houses. One is immediately struck by the clarity of the composition and the excellent use of complementary colours.

Several details show the care that has been taken. The range has to relate to both the two-storey terrace and the taller church, so the section nearest the houses is lowered. Then the height of the main range is modified by the use of a band of red brick across the yellow to emphasize the horizontal as against the vertical. Consider how different the façade would be without it; if the two blocks of colour simply met, the effect would be heavier and the sense of horizontal direction would be lost. There is a further point about the brick. The colours refer to both the red brick church and the pale brick terrace, providing a transition from one to the other. Thus at the church end of the building the red seems to dominate, while at the other end one is more aware of the yellow. There is even a gable parapet to echo the one at the east end of the church. In short, these details are not there by a whim or accident. This is good, considerate design.

Passing over Mill Road bridge one cannot but be struck by the chimneys of the cottages on the left. Their height was practical to take the smoke from coal fires above the level of the bridge, but the visual effect is delightfully picturesque. The trees here make a stunning impression, particularly when in leaf. How different from the barren landscape around Hills Road bridge.

*A hint of grand Tudor architecture pervades these 19th-century cottages, with their artfully arranged chimneys.*

Then on the right, in quick succession, come two more remarkable buildings. The former Mill Road Branch Library was built in 1897 to a design by Frank Walters, and it closed exactly one hundred years later, despite a local campaign to keep it open. Though listed, it has been horribly neglected and disfigured. The original top lighting – a kind of long glass lantern running the length of the roof-ridge – has been boarded up in the crudest fashion, like the clumsy replacement fascias one sees at railway stations such as March. There are wonderful details in terracotta and stone, demonstrating the pride the Victorians felt in creating such civic amenities: the date in the pediment above the entrance is crowned to mark the year of Queen Victoria's Diamond Jubilee, while two lions in age-blackened red stone, flanking the pediment, hold shields of the borough arms. Renaissance-style features decorate the upper façade and the roof is topped by a shapely lantern and cupola. Happily the interior is in much better condition, having been refurbished by the Indian Culture and Community Association to create the Bharat Bhavan community centre.

*Mill Road Branch Library, completed in Queen Victoria's Diamond Jubilee year.*

*Mill Road Branch Library's panache and exuberant detailing express pride and confidence in Victorian civic values.*

On the corner of Gwydir Street lies the old Bath House (1927), perfectly placed and proportioned. It too displays civic pride, with full-colour arms above the entrance. The photos on this page speak for themselves. It is a shame that the street furniture gets in the way, particularly the ugly phone booth and the cable junction box. And is there really a need for the disfiguring burglar alarm? No one ever pays a ringing alarm the slightest attention. It might also have been a kindness if Lifecraft had limited itself to one sign, especially given the strident yellow it favours. These are the little niceties that make all the difference.

Further on we come to Ditchburn Place (1838), once the maternity hospital and before that a workhouse. It is now sheltered accommodation for the elderly, a benign version of its original function. It was built at a time when good proportions seem to have been normal, but sadly it is rare for any building to retain its original appearance in the way the architect conceived it. Additions, expansions and alterations will all tend to dislocate a scheme unless they are very carefully done – or even if they *are* carefully done. Here, two wings have been added at different times and with the features of their particular day.

*Left and above: Civic provision for the great unwashed - the former Mill Road Bath House, opened in 1927.*

Although in some ways trying to harmonise, they are predictably taller than the original building and upset its composition. The southeast wing is the more recent and the less satisfactory, with gaping modern windows. The northwest wing has better fenestration, but features an ugly staircase tower that faces the road and shows too much glass. Its flat top is inappropriate for a building that should properly end in a gable. The front courtyard contains an intrusive shed and is, possibly, overplanted with trees. These screen but also obscure what is still, despite the faults just mentioned, a very pleasing building.

All these buildings are impressive examples of 19th- and early 20th-century civic provision for local residents. On a less ambitious scale, there is also something impressive about the parade of shops between Devonshire Road and St Barnabas Road. The flats above them carry on up boldly into large dormers of the same size as the first-floor windows, a grand gesture that defies their modest status. Even the bogus half-timbering seems to cut a dash. One would be sorry if these were swept away.

*Above: The northwest wing of Ditchburn Place, viewed from Mill Road.*

*Right: An eye-catching parade of shops between Devonshire Road and St Barnabas Road.*

**127**

Of course there is much that is ugly in Mill Road, particularly wherever the building line is set back. Avis and the Cambridge Bed Centre, useful though they are, do not bring architectural distinction to the road. The Broadway has the Co-op's insensitive signage running the whole length of several buildings, where signs should be needed only above the two entrances. The building now occupied by Tesco Express is a particularly nasty bit of infill, entirely disregarding its neighbours with an utterly unimaginative and basic façade. Its ground floor and first floor bear no relation to each other at all.

*Crass infill on the Broadway.*

On the town side of the bridge, Scholars House (another of those pretentious names, and suffering from apostrophe amnesia) inspires mixed feelings. The stair turret carries a nice reference to the old Kinema picture house it replaced, using an Art Deco style common in cinemas of the 1930s. The recessed entrance is narrow but inviting, one wall angled to allow the curved approach a pedestrian is unconsciously inclined to take, and the two recessed windows on the ground floor are a nice touch. The upper windows, however, are plain to the point of bleakness. This is a neat building, yet somehow not entirely convincing.

*Facing page*

*Top and centre top: Scholars House.*

*Top right: Retail unit on the site of a former garage.*

*Bottom: The façade of the old Playhouse in the 1930s (left), replaced in the 1960s by concrete and mosaic (right).*

There can be no doubt about the building on the corner of Covent Garden. This is one of the vilest in the whole of Cambridge. Paradoxically, it used to have one of Mill Road's more exuberant – not to say astonishing – frontages when it was the Playhouse, Cambridge's first purpose-built cinema. This was opened in 1913, and when they closed it for good over fifty years later, the owners removed the playful front in its entirety. During the 1960s and 1970s it was a Fine Fare supermarket, a period of its history that still lives on in mosaic tiling and concrete render. It is now occupied by Sally Ann's charity shop.

*The gaping porte-cochère of Petersfield Mansions*

*Below: A pitched-roofed council-house lookalike nestles incongruously against the corner tower like an asbestos-clad afterthought.*

At the very end of the road stands Petersfield Mansions, which replaced the postal sorting office in 1993. Stylistically it makes some reference to the Art Deco style, with horizontal glazing bars and a monumental tower at the corner, but the building is heavy, the windows crude and oversized, and the Mill Road frontage ungainly and confusing. The *porte-cochère* is draughty looking, affording too great a view of parked cars, the distant far side of the development and even the sky. It makes the floor above appear unanchored, uncomfortably suspended above a void, the vast size of the window seeming to require a more substantial foundation than this gaping hole. There are some attractive details – the pillared porches, the windows with stone surrounds and the nicely stepped tower. Unfortunately, the effect of the latter is complicated by the addition of what resembles a council house made from prefabricated panels, which perches next to it like an after-thought. The confusion is increased by an obviously pitched roof where the style of the whole building seems to invite a flat one, or at least a concealed pitch. The attempts to vary the façade have made it fussy and busy. This is a shame, for it is on a particularly conspicuous site. Seen across Donkey Common, however, the effect is less troublesome as trees do their usual work of softening the impact.

*Human-scale Seymour Court, now demolished.*

*Below: Three- and four-storey Trinity Mews under construction.*

The side streets in Romsey are Coronation-Street dull, and one might think that new developments would be welcomed. Sadly that is not always the case. It seems to be characteristic of our time that new schemes often threaten rather than enhance a neighbourhood, with quiet corners being imposed upon by overbearing, high-density housing in unsympathetic styles and materials. A current example can be found where Seymour Street winds behind Brookfields Hospital. The story is typical and instructive. This was once a pleasant haven for the elderly: on one corner, in leafy surroundings, Brook House, an old people's home; on the other, Seymour Court, a group of low red-brick, warden-controlled flats attractively laid out like a college around intimate and secluded green courts. Although they were barely forty years old, the flats were becoming shabby and, consisting as they did of small bedsitters, were no longer popular nor easily upgradable to modern requirements. Nowadays the council does not maintain, refurbish or rebuild such properties. Instead it sells up, moves residents on, and invites private developers in. The standard deal is for a site to be divided, with the developer constructing new but fewer flats for the council while profiting from the creation and sale of luxury homes. A publicly owned asset is thereby diminished, and accommodation for the elderly and vulnerable reduced.

Kier Group, working closely with the council, produced initial designs of shocking scale and ugliness; the computer-generated image in the News and Crier (29 September 2011) showed a stark, jumbled composition with a frightful metal-clad four-storey 'landmark' feature on the narrow corner. This provoked strong complaints from residents. Said one: 'What is proposed is an extraordinarily massive building to be putting in a side street and it's completely unprecedented ... (it) overlooks and overbears everything in the surrounding area.' Kier Group's response was predictably cavalier: 'Cambridge is a vibrant city where strong architecture is encouraged and the contemporary design and materials reflect this.' Almost every word begs a question. What is a 'vibrant' city? Glitzy and nasty? What is 'strong architecture'? Aggressively ugly? Who is 'encouraging' it? And with what mandate to do so? And what is 'contemporary design' – a synonym for gimmicky?

The designs were modified and, while taller buildings have not been eliminated, they have been scaled down and the metal cladding removed. But one developers' trick has not been knocked on the head. The local reference has been dispensed with; the address is no longer Seymour Court. You won't be surprised by its fatuous new name – Trinity Mews.

*Tom Amey Court - a modern interpretation of the traditional terrace.*

*The former site of the Jubilee Tavern, now occupied by the respectful pastiche of Jubilee Terrace. The entire corner replicates features of the original building.*

There are better examples of redevelopment, such as those in St Philip's Road. Tom Amey Court (1989) sits well on the corner of Ross Street, and the more recent Jubilee Terrace by Catharine Street is a good example of respectful pastiche that seems to fit better than any attempt to be ultra-modern. Devonshire Road has a similar modern terrace very thoughtfully composed and well proportioned (see photo overleaf), whose roofline exactly matches that of the adjacent terrace. The doors and bay windows are symmetrically positioned and grouped to very satisfying effect, with the bays running up to the roof and the dormers placed above them. This arrangement, with two bays side by side in the centre, creates two wide areas of blank pale brick. On the ground floor this space is relieved by the entrances, round-arched and conveniently recessed for shelter. Above the arches runs a band of red brick in three courses, to lend variety to the façade and to re-state the horizontal line of the range as against the vertical direction of the four tall bays and dormers. Below the eaves, in the exact centre, is a perfect touch of detail in a little red-brick, stepped bracket which neatly punctuates the expanse of golden brickwork.

*Harmonious and thoughtful
infill on Devonshire Road.*

This terrace makes good use of the roof space by introducing dormers, thereby creating a third storey without being overbearing, unlike its opposite number at Ravensworth Gardens. It is a triumph of attention to detail and shows the importance of relating harmoniously to existing buildings. It does not draw immediate attention to itself, except for its newness and cleanness. Yet, unlike much that we see around the station, it is a building of marked distinction.

The Mill Road area is still fundamentally mean, though no longer squalid. Yet it has sufficient merit to make it more attractive to the young buyers I have spoken to than the flats by the railway line, which says something about the kind of 'progress' made in the last hundred years. Wholesale redevelopment, were it still possible, would not be desirable. There are worthwhile buildings here that should not be lost either actually through demolition or visually through being swamped by unsympathetic housing developments of the kind we have often seen in recent times. Careful piece-meal rebuilding as the opportunity arises, and with firm guiding principles, is the better option. In particular, there should be no overcrowding, and an avoidance of developers with a track record of increasing the scale of their schemes once they have jammed a foot in the door.

## 6

# New Town and Barnwell: early redevelopment

New Town, as its name suggests, was one of the earliest building developments to follow the Enclosure Acts. It was also one of the first to be redeveloped in the 20th century. Barnwell likewise underwent substantial redevelopment from the 1960s onwards.

## New Town

New Town was laid out piecemeal by different landowners between c. 1820 and 1850, and the quality of building varied depending upon their intentions. The better housing survives along the boundaries of the Town; on Brookside and Panton Street to the west, on Lensfield Road to the north, and on Bateman Street and Norwich Street to the south. The eastern boundary is marked by the shops and offices of Hills Road. Within that perimeter, inferior dwellings built as a poor quarter have largely been replaced. The area to the south of Saxon Street was attracting unfavourable comment as early as 1850, and by 1950 the Holford Report regarded this high density 'third class' housing as nearing the end of its useful life. A photograph in the report (Vol. 1, facing p. 41) shows the view from St Paul's Church tower over what might be the opening credits to 'Coronation Street' – and ironically there is a Coronation Street in New Town too.

*The eight-storey Hanover Court, viewed from Coronation Street.*

Much of the warren of houses and workshops in this area has been swept away, but there are interesting survivals; short terraces which were deemed fit to remain or which, for one reason or another, the council could not acquire or afford to develop. The result is a surprisingly interesting, if messy, area, which might not have been the case had a grand plan been imposed. Part of such a plan can be seen at Hanover Court and Princess Court, which lie between Coronation Street and Union Road. The area where they stand, bounded on the east by George IV Street and on the west by Bentinck Street, contained some of the worst of the old slums. When they were cleared away, the paramount concern was to let in light and air, and blocks of flats were seen as the answer, since they would allow high density of occupation while simultaneously creating open space.

The first sight of Hanover Court is unexpected; despite its height of eight storeys, it is not visible from many of the nearby streets, nor from Trumpington Road or Hills Road. One would like to know if there had been any deliberate calculation of the adjacent sight lines. It is strange to think that something so large can be tucked away unseen.

The tree-dotted garden between it and five-storey Princess Court makes for a peaceful setting, but one would not have wanted the intended multiplication of these barrack blocks. The balconied living rooms face west in both cases, so those of the taller Hanover Court look across at the bleak back of Princess Court. Since the latter contains bedrooms and bathrooms where light is less important, more tree screening could have been employed here. George IV Street, for example, is protected in this way from Hanover Court's dull east side.

To the north, the development presents its ugliest side to Union Road – the wall of the car park that serves both tower blocks. Part, however, is mercifully screened by Virginia creeper. Union Road itself is uninviting, a confusion of styles and brick colours; the Perse Girls' School has put up a new classroom block in dark red brick, where surrounding houses are in the once-standard yellow-grey of Victorian Cambridge. Though neat and well proportioned, its colour makes it notably incongruous.

*Above: The west-facing façade of Hanover Court.*

*Below: the blank wall of the car park serving Hanover Court and Princess Court, Union Road.*

*A miscellany of materials on the corner of Bentinck Street and Union Road - a traditional yellow-brick terrace, the Perse Girls' School in red brick, and the metal-clad Chemistry Laboratory extension.*

*Beyond utilitarianism - the finely-detailed statue on the belfry of St Alban's schoolhouse.*

Three buildings stand out in this road. The first is the much-criticised Chemistry Laboratory (1953-60), massive, overbearing and an abomination in the context of Lensfield Road. The southern façade, looking across the rear car park to Union Road, has had a recent face-lift. Whether or not this improves matters depends on one's taste for modern statements. The green 'chimneys' are a mixed blessing to the Cambridge skyline, but perhaps we shall get used to them.

The second building of note, in yellow brick and blue slate, is St Alban's Catholic Primary School (pictured on the following page), a delightful example of the Victorian approach to scholastic buildings. It presents an attractive composition to the street, simple but varied and of human scale, an increasing rarity these days. It also displays those little touches of thoughtful detail which we see so often on Victorian buildings, such as the occasional decorative use of different coloured brick, as on the west gable, or the dogtooth pattern under the sill running below the three central windows. It has twice been successfully extended to the west, so discreetly that it takes a second glance to realise this (look at the gable end and the plinth in the top photograph overleaf).

*This page: Two views of St. Alban's Primary School, Union Road.*

*Top: View from the west, showing the two careful extensions.*

*Bottom: View from the east.*

*Facing page*

*Left column: Decorative brickwork - details from the Crystallographic Data Centre (top), the Unilever Centre for Molecular Informatics (centre) and St Alban's School (bottom).*

*Right: The Unilever Centre for Molecular Informatics.*

But the real gem in this street is Erik Sørensen's unpretentious Crystallographic Data Centre (1992), described in Chapter 4. This well-bred, understated building is hugely impressive and one of the finest modern buildings in Cambridge.

Sørensen also designed the Unilever Centre for Molecular Informatics (1999), which stands at the other end of the Chemistry Laboratory. Though not perhaps quite as impressive – the little triangular bay windows do not wholly convince – it nonetheless displays the same well-judged proportions and skilfully punctuated expanses of clean brickwork. The windows at ground level are especially eye-catching, resembling the profile of a crow-stepped gable topped by a chimney, their outlines as sharp as if made by a giant pastry cutter. The bricks are of conventional shape, unlike those of the Crystallographic Data Centre, and their colour matches that of the adjacent Chemistry Laboratory. Blind windows and doors create additional relief and interest. And in another characteristic touch, the triangular drainpipes of both buildings are set into recesses in the walls.

Lensfield Road, the northern edge of New Town, contains the fine Roman Catholic Church and the delightful Scott Polar Institute, with its new library skilfully added in a far more attractive style than the earlier extension at the back.

The out-of-scale Chemistry Laboratory follows, then Downing Terrace, whose façade is as elegant as one would expect for its period (1819), with the exception of the centrepiece, where scale and proportion are not right. The rear view of the terrace from Saxon Street reveals unexpected ugliness, however. Picture windows have been inserted of a kind that one would have expected to be banned from such buildings (Grade II listed), and in 2009 the adjacent Lensfield Hotel gained permission to add modernist cube-like extensions, despite protests that they were out of keeping with its Regency style. The hotel's rear elevation certainly needed tidying up, and the new extensions, though incongruous, have proved better than feared.

The western side of New Town contains several attractive corners around Panton Street and St Eligius Street. Russell Court, to the east of Panton Street, comprises modern buildings of a human scale and intimacy, with varied rooflines and façades. There are unusual corners and intriguing little vistas that reduce a large development into comfortable small components. In a courtyard garden one unexpectedly finds two upright stone dragons supporting shields. A melancholy reminder of a time when the Royal Mail played a greater and more dignified role in human affairs, they used to stand on the old post office in Petty Cury, and were brought here after it was demolished in the late 1960s. Panton Street itself mostly consists of its original 19th-century housing, which comprises buildings of different heights, seemingly put up piecemeal but of broadly similar style; the overall effect is a pleasant one, even if St Mary's School, closing the view at the southern end, is too domineering for its position. One or two houses have been cleaned up to a startling raw yellow, particularly stark against those which retain the grey weathering of age. Unless dirt actually damages the brick, it is hard to see a need to clean it off; it is not as if one were restoring golden Oxford stone.

To the south of the area, Norwich Street runs interminably long, dull and monotonous, composed of inferior houses whose proximity to the railway and the city centre gives them price tags far in excess of their intrinsic merits. Bateman Street is largely unchanged except at the eastern end where Eurocentres Cambridge intrudes, a building almost industrial in appearance, clad in drab beige panels and guarded by a fashionable fence of metal poles and wires. The houses on the south side of the street are better than the taller, gaunt terraces opposite, but numbers of them have been converted to offices, sometimes with a bridge connecting two villas. This kind of thing happens in suburbs that are too close to the town centre for their own good.

*Above: The engaging new extension to the Scott Polar Institute.*

*Below: The old Post Office dragons - an unexpected touch of whimsy in Russell Court.*

*Top: Half-millionaires' Row -
grotesquely overpriced
workers' cottages in the
monotonous terrace of
Norwich Street.*

*Bottom: The Eurocentres
Cambridge building  -
corporate scale and industrial
materials disrupt Bateman
Street.*

# Barnwell

Like New Town, Barnwell has been redeveloped, in part piecemeal and in part according to large schemes (not fully realised). There is a variety of buildings old and new, some good sensibly scaled infill, some ancient survivals (the remains of Barnwell Priory and the Leper Chapel) and a surprising number of trees.

The biggest area of new development is that formerly known as the Kite. Despite the fact that it was the slummiest part of Barnwell, with narrow streets of mean buildings packed tightly together, there was considerable public opposition to plans for its renewal, which involved the construction of a shopping complex. This was meant to relieve pressure on Cambridge's historic centre, but in the event did nothing of the kind; people simply visited both and produced an incessant flow of pedestrians across Christ's Pieces and New Square. The complex, named the Grafton Centre, was an early example of shopping under cover in what is now peculiarly called a 'mall'.

What are the chief features of this mall? The entrances are small, allowing the place to be locked up at night – thus the whole area becomes a giant shop in itself. Several streets were obliterated or truncated to make way for it, and one's freedom to roam the area they used to occupy is now severely curtailed; once the shops have closed there is no way through. A limited right of way has been retained through Lion Yard, Cambridge's first mall, but it too is considered private property; anyone attempting to take photographs there will be confronted in a trice by 'security guards' and will be read a petty tyrant's version of the Riot Act. Private retail, with its CCTV cameras ever on the lookout for 'undesirables', has taken over what was once, at least in part, public space.

The approach to the Grafton Centre from East Road has already been mentioned in Chapter 2. One enters as into a castle, through a small aperture in a bleak façade and into a tunnel-like passage. Security rather than entice-ment is paramount here, the latter perhaps considered unnecessary in an age of crazed consumerism. There is nothing to suggest the experience ahead or the goods on offer, a very great contrast to the market square with its open stalls and traditional form of concentrated shopping. Although this is the place where buses and taxis drop off, it is very much the back door.

*Crispin Place (above) and Burleigh Place (below), former thoroughfares truncated and privatised.*

*The Fitzroy Street entrance to the Grafton Centre.*

The main entrance, on Fitzroy Street, is every bit as mean as the other. It was later revamped with glass canopies in an attempt to make it more exciting, and the result is catastrophic. With arches cut in half and of random heights, the conception looks unfinished – a cheap conservatory botched up by cowboy builders who couldn't read the plans. Its three coloured 'kites' (the allusion is not immediately obvious) impertinently refer to the old popular name for the area, The Kite, whose preservation was a local *cause célèbre* during the 1970s. The structure jars against the more obvious focus of the street, the former Eden Chapel whose balanced façade automatically draws the eye. This Grafton greenhouse looks wrong, as if it should not be there, or as if it were temporarily left by the cowboys while they work out how to assemble the kit correctly. The bogus mateyness of dropping 'Centre' and calling the place 'The Grafton' adds insult to injury. People might casually call it that, but it isn't necessary to rename it in consequence. One doesn't see 'Emma' appearing on Emmanuel College notepaper.

Inside, things are not so bad. A café is placed invitingly near the entrance. A broad corridor of shops opens out into a wider square, then leads on to a full-height atrium with a gallery of other shops, more cafés and a cinema. Alas, the shops contain almost nothing anyone would want unless it is women's fashion, beauty products or mobile phones.

Fitzroy Street and Burleigh Street, which bound the Grafton Centre on the southeast, have both been partly redeveloped. Their pedestrianisation is welcome, as is the attractively patterned circle of cobbles where they meet, showing the points of the compass. The paving as a whole is better and more coherent than that of the city centre (see Chapter 3). The two streets display a variety of styles and periods, not especially distinguished but more reassuring than a complete rebuild – compare King Street, for instance.

The most notable feature of Fitzroy Street is the old Laurie and McConnell store with its rooftop bandstand. This is a building of real distinction, beautifully proportioned and detailed – and of course spoilt, like so many shops, by a complete disjunction between its ground floor and its upper storeys. There is little visual continuity between the two, and the vast plate-glass windows almost remove any sense of a ground floor at all, giving it a gutted or unfinished look when contrasted with the solidity of the brick and stonework above. This is a common fault which a great many towns in Denmark have successfully remedied, and it is time it was remedied here. (See for example Peter Olesen's 'Paenere Facader' [Thaning and Appel 2005]; you don't have to read Danish – the photos speak for themselves.)

*The former Laurie and McConnell building, its street-level frontage totally at odds with the floors above.*

*The visually jarring Fitzroy Street - a collision of periods and styles.*

*Crass and boorish, this Brutalist box disregards the scale of old Burleigh Street.*

The buildings either side of the old store display the mediocrity of several periods – to the left a glass box dating from the 1960s, to the right a clumsy 1980s barn of a building with heavy balconies and a messy roof. Next to it stands a relentlessly horizontal row of shops, flat roofed, with a diamond-patterned brick façade and ugly windows characteristic of the 1950s, and reminiscent of the now demolished Bradwell's Court. Not one makes any attempt to connect with its neighbours, and the effect is not picturesque, as it sometimes can be, but jarring. The opposite side of the road consists of nondescript 1990s novelties, hopelessly drab.

In Burleigh Street more of the older shops survive, two-storeyed, comfortable and uninvasive, even though many have atrocious signage, pram-hood blinds, ill-matched ground-floor frontages and similar irritants. There is one especially reprehensible intrusion of modern Brutalism (shown above) behind the Cancer Research charity shop: a brick and concrete box with staring windows and a flat roof disfigured by untidy aerials, mini-boxes and other perplexing clutter. The deplorable skyline it produces was no doubt once considered smart and cutting edge. It is, of course, taller than its neighbours, following the unwritten rule that any new building must be bigger than its predecessor.

*Roskilde, Denmark - shop fronts harmoniously integrated into the façade of a building.*

**145**

The newest here rise up even taller into veritable temples of Mammon. On one side we have Primark, 21st-century Smart and quite out of keeping with the street's 19th-century cottage-like shops. New buildings invariably display some gimmick or other, so here we find odd projections between the windows like venetian blinds, and what looks like a row of skis jutting from the parapet of the roof, a feature seen elsewhere and already a cliché. Does it serve any practical purpose?

Facing Primark we have the southwest side of the Grafton Centre, whose façade is neither one thing nor another. Its overall appearance and general proportions are safe and dull, with an attempt to refer to the former chapel, to which it is connected, by the use of round-arched entrance door and windows, highlighted in lighter-coloured brick. But modish details must not be omitted, so there is a daft tent-like canopy over the entrance. This is a mystery. It is pitched in such a way as to invite the wind and rain underneath rather than intercept them, and it is too high to offer any real protection, any more than if you held a handkerchief above your head. It seems to be nothing more than a symbol of up-to-date credentials – unless it is a safety net for the ski-jumpers on Primark's roof.

*This page: Human-scale 1960s redevelopment in Barnwell by David Roberts.*

To the east of the Grafton Centre lie several areas of substantial redevelopment. Some remain commercial zones, new trading estates like Coral Park which have replaced older workshops and warehouses, and which are mostly every bit as dreary as you would expect. Others have been given over to intensive housing developments, the earliest of which pre-dates the Grafton Centre by twenty-five years.

The triangle between East Road, Norfolk Street and St Matthew's Street was the first major slum clearance in Cambridge, begun in 1959 and designed by architect David Roberts. It is what would now be called 'social housing', that ludicrous euphemism which makes matters worse by association with social security and benefits. In 1959 it was more accurately called low-cost housing. It has many merits: low-rise blocks are arranged around large courts, open, green and airy in contrast to the warren of houses and workshops they replaced. Each block is made up of maisonettes, all of which have living rooms aligned to face the sun. Those on the ground floor have small walled gardens, and there are communal green areas too, with mature trees transplanted to augment pre-existing ones. Unlike some of the more recent large housing developments in the area, this one retains a human scale and an intimacy of layout that also secures privacy.

The prospect from East Road is visually less successful. The architect rightly kept the buildings turned away from the road as far as possible, but the result is an unsettling street frontage, with little plots of lost, neglected ground between each angled building. In fairness it is difficult to see how else to deal with the proximity to such a busy, noisy road. An additional flaw is that the universal ownership of cars was not anticipated, and so there are too few garages – not that people would necessarily use them were they provided. In consequence, the open spaces, which could be made to look more attractive and cared for, are despoiled in the all-too-usual manner by parked cars. The development looks a little shabby now, and the public gardens are dull and neglected; some better planting and maintenance would make a difference.

A more recent development of substance is the three-sided court of St Matthew's Gardens, lying off York Street and Abbey Walk. It has attempted to harmonise with the character of the area in respect of brick colour, sash windows, pitched roofs and 'chimneys', and in places one is reminded of Poundbury in Dorset, but the scale of the construction is different. Tall three-storey ranges enclose a vast green space, big enough for a football or cricket pitch but almost certainly intended for neither, which covers an underground car park – a neat solution to the visual pollution of the ubiquitous motor car. For all its attempts to fit in, however, St Matthews Gardens lacks the intimacy of the nearby Victorian streets. In fact, the initial impression it makes is almost Stalinist, like so many new developments.

*This page: St Matthew's Gardens, with its vast scale, verges on the megalomanic.*

There is a kind of megalomania in these colossal constructions, an echo of Soviet Russia's huge hives for the masses, 'the People', 'the Toilers of the Nation', though any worker wanting a home here will need a large salary to afford it; proletarians need not apply.

While not as large as St Matthew's Gardens, Grebe Court, on the corner of Garlic Row and Oyster Row, is another example of over-development that bulks unpleasantly. Its architecture is not bad, but it is three storeys tall, and visible – as it should not be – from the riverside below; developments of this type would be so much better were they less densely built.

Smaller rebuilding projects have been more thoughtful and intelligent. Vicarage Terrace (with fine trees over the old wall of the vicarage – one might be in a village) contains a red-brick range by Granta Housing. Superficially it is nothing special, but the windows are generously sized, and the integral recessed porches are far more practical than the more common, and less visually pleasing, tacked-on canopies seen elsewhere. River Lane, to the north of Newmarket Road, has a mix of old and new terraces, the recent additions also having sheltered porches. There are signs

*The Granta Housing scheme in Vicarage Terrace.*

**149**

that more builders, especially smaller firms putting up just three or four houses, are prepared to take some trouble over design, with results that are modest and simple, and which display just the right touch of detail to provide distinction. This is very much to be welcomed in older areas. New Street, for example, has some very good new terraces in clean, light brick that are well proportioned, in harmony with its older properties, and possess features such as round-arched doorways that lend them a touch of class.

*This 21st-century development in New Street takes a 19th-century formula and brings it up to date, resulting in comfortable, human-scale homes.*

New Town and Barnwell have seen redevelopment on both the large and the small scale. In general, larger-scale rebuilding has failed to produce good results, chiefly because of the imperative to pack in as much as possible and the difficulties of giving coherence or distinction to monolithic façades. By comparison, the older streets in the two areas seem less monotonous – with the exception of the interminable York Street – and recent smaller-scale rebuilding has often been done with notable sensitivity and an eye for quality.

**7**

# The outer suburbs

'God almighty first planted a garden...' (Bacon, 'Of Gardens', 1625)

Suburban used to be a term of abuse, and perhaps it still is. Suburbs were considered dull, respectable, 'Pooterish', the abode of those not grand enough to own good town houses or retreats in the country. Suburban has been a synonym for provincial, narrow minded, boring. Yet something like half the population of this country lives in the suburbs, and now that young people are increasingly compelled to live in flats, owning a suburban semi-detached house on a decent-sized plot is once again an aspiration – to be surrounded by trees with their blossom in spring, to be very little overlooked, to have a garden of one's own. Consequently, even modest houses in the early garden suburbs now command high prices beyond the reach of the working class for whom they were built. However, the desirability of suburbia is being eroded by creeping urbanisation, conversion of houses to other uses, growing population density, garden grabbing, over-development and the building of ugly extensions.

The most obviously visible sign of this erosion is the garden grabbing, and particularly the demolition of family houses to make way for blocks of flats. As flat dwelling becomes more acceptable to councils anxious to meet government housing targets, so planning permission is given to developers looking to make a killing. Dormitory barracks for commuters not only rise up on ugly brownfield sites by the railway, but also make unwelcome appearances in suburban gardens.

*Sedley Taylor Road - Cambridge suburbia at its most accomplished.*

The development of Wessex Court in Queen Edith's Way shows what happens. One day your neighbouring property is a detached house in a large garden, the next it is fourteen apartments. That means quite possibly twenty-eight cars or more and multiple comings and goings; more people, more vehicles, more tarmac, more noise, less greenery. People have to live somewhere, but surely not packed together like sardines on someone's former lawn. Most of the front lawn here is now given over to car parking, paving slabs, gravel and electronic gates, bringing an unwelcome urban aspect to the plot. To be fair, the design of these apartments ('traditionally built in a contemporary style' by Wheatley) is striking and interesting enough, but the development is in the wrong place; wrong visually, wrong in relation to its neighbours, wrong in its height, wrong in its density of occupation. That concerns the developers not at all; 'similar properties required' says the board outside. Before long there will be apartment blocks on roundabouts.

At one time there were philanthropic housing idealists, like George Cadbury or Ebenezer Howard. Cadbury believed in the therapeutic – even moral – advantages of gardens, and insisted that no house should occupy more than

*The changing face of suburbia - two family homes were demolished to make way for the 14 apartments of this gated community at Wessex Court, Queen Edith's Way.*

*The suburban ideal - a detached house in well-tended gardens; Sun House, the splendid Art Deco neighbour to Wessex Court.*

a quarter of its plot. As a result Bournville became, and remains to this day, one of the most desirable suburbs in Birmingham. But a hundred years on, the crudely speculative developer is still with us. Maximum profit and minimum green space remain the order of the day. Why did the Queen Edith's Way development stop at fourteen flats when there must have been room for more? Perhaps because fourteen is the limit beyond which 'social housing' is required of the developer. In contrast to George Cadbury's philosophy, this development could hardly appear more cynical; it seems to have been restrained not by social conscience but by planning law.

Glebe Road has been badly hit. One block of flats went up some years ago, then in 1998 Perse School House was sold, along with the large field behind it. This former school boarding house was once the home of distinguished headmaster and classical scholar Dr W.H.D. Rouse, and contained a fine purpose-built library for his vast personal collection. It was demolished in 2000 and replaced by an entire close of 'executive homes'. However, some social housing was built on the street front, and the mature trees on the site were left unmolested.

*From back garden to closed compound - the Maison Verre in Glebe Road.*

Then in 2009 Glebe Road saw an astonishing example of garden grabbing. Lavishly appointed Maison Verre ('Glasshouse' or 'Greenhouse') applied the concept of building a 'green' house that would need very little or no conventional heating, and was marketed for a staggering £1.5 million. Yet, built in a modest suburban back garden abutting the top stretch of the road, it possesses no proper garden of its own, and has a number of rooms situated underground. There is absolutely no outlook, as it is surrounded by a high wall. It must be the most expensive bunker/hothouse in Cambridge. It came onto the market again very soon after it was first sold, apparently because its much-vaunted 'greenhouse effect' (*l'effet de la Maison Verre*) tended to fry the occupants. Whereas most suburban houses are open in aspect, this one, with its vast windows, necessarily hides away behind a blank wall like a Roman house in densely urban Pompeii. In a spacious suburban road it is an anomaly. It would have been even more so had the developer been able to get the planning permission he wanted for anything higher than a single storey.

Redevelopment struck again in Glebe Road two years later. Early in 2011, a fairly standard, cottage-like, garden-suburb detached house in brick and render was demolished to make way for a modern house so tall that at first it was assumed to be a block of flats. The completed building is quite out of keeping with the character of the road and the whole area. How did the

*Though necessary for those who live in glass houses, a wall such as this is totally out of place in the open setting of Glebe Road.*

planners let this through? Why did they limit Maison Verre to one storey, yet allow three here? Early on in its construction, one passerby said it appeared as though a spaceship had landed. The building could not be more at odds with its neighbour, seeming to threaten the latter's demolition as three tilting roof-slabs look ready to slide down onto it. The roofline is well above the chimneys of the adjacent house and also projects further forward, making it visible from far down the road. Its materials are 'Contemporary Cliché'. It couldn't care less about fitting in. Such houses – brash buildings one might expect to see on a brownfield site – are destroying the ambience of mature suburbs.

Later that year, another perfectly good Glebe Road house was demolished on account of its spacious garden. The developers originally gained planning permission for two 'executive homes', to be offered for £2.5 million each; having got that far, they put in a further application for ten flats, a tactic all too familiar. Permission for a similar development nearby was refused some years ago, on the grounds that it would worsen traffic congestion in a road that already suffers from Addenbrooke's parking and contains a pre-preparatory school with its daily Chelsea tractor deliveries. This new development is directly opposite the school. Fortunately, sense seems to have prevailed and just the two 'luxury' houses were built in a vernacular style that respects the others in the road.

*In its height, scale, materials and style, this new development displays a total disregard for the established character of Glebe Road. Where, one has to ask, were the planners when this was approved?*

One of the ways in which suburbia is being degraded - a muddy car park for a small business replaces the lawns and hedges of a garden.

There has been a further creeping urbanisation as houses are turned into business premises, something that began to happen in the inner suburbs some time ago. Rambling Victorian houses designed for large families with resident servants became inconvenient and expensive to run, and were converted to flats, offices or small private schools. The trend has now spread to the outer suburbs. Small businesses, dental practices, guest houses and so on are set up in what were originally family homes, bringing with them signage, logos, car parking and increased traffic. They bring garden grabbing too. When a house is no longer a home, the garden is not needed and becomes either a car park, like this deplorable example above, or another house, as seen in the example of Glebe Road's 'greenhouse'.

When houses become offices one can at least expect corporate pride and business sense to ensure a well-maintained frontage. The opposite happens when two related factors are considered, the increase of 'buy-to-let' and the spread of growing numbers of students throughout the community. Not so long ago there was only one university in Cambridge. It accommodated its students in colleges or else in approved lodgings, mostly in college-owned properties. Then the government thought that it would be a good idea if up to fifty per cent of teenagers went to a university. (Why stop at fifty?) After two or three years of more book-learning they would emerge with 'skills' that would benefit the economy. The consequence has been a huge expansion of student numbers – especially in the new universities, which have a vested interest in taking as many students as they are allowed, both to prove that they are 'successful' and to obtain more funds. They also need to cover the drop-out rate which inevitably accompanies an academically weak cohort. Numbers have risen well beyond the capacity of the universities to house them. These institutions look to private landlords to take the overflow which now reaches to the outer suburbs.

This has encouraged the 'buy-to-let' phenomenon. There is money to be made from renting out as many bed-sitters as can be fashioned from a house, so perfectly good family homes in quiet suburbs are converted for student use. Revenue can be further increased by building annexes in the back gardens. Some will say this is perfectly laudable enterprise. Neighbours may well call it something else, for they will be the ones experiencing noise at unsociable hours. The gardens, when not built on, will be weed-choked for eleven months at a time until the landlord blitzes them at the end of the academic year, and since students seem to live on alcohol and takeaways, there will be unfeasible amounts of packaging tumbling out of bins which the binmen will refuse to empty on Health and Safety grounds. And no young person ever closes a front door quietly.

A student house can easily be picked out in any residential street, like a boil on a neck. This is not to say that students are some sort of noxious under-class, but their irregular hours, carefree lifestyle and cavalier attitude to the niceties of household management mean that they fit uncomfortably into conventional suburban life, and unwittingly contribute to the erosion of suburban amenity. As a former student and now a 'respectable' suburban dweller who mows his lawn twice a week, I can appreciate both sides of the problem. Ideally students would live in well-defined areas or in college, but if that cannot be achieved the suburbs will continue to suffer.

As if that weren't sufficiently tiresome, there is the wider problem of 'houses in multiple occupation' – a term which includes student houses but also refers to those shared by young professionals and migrants. In April 2012, Labour Councillor Gail Marchant-Daisley, who represents Petersfield, proposed a limit of 25% on the number of HMOs in any street, suggesting that too many homes in multiple occupation damaged community spirit and increased the resemblance to a commuter town. She said she

*Property agents are keen to let suburban homes to students, as houses in multiple occupation yield higher rents on aggregate. Neighbours tend not to find this arrangement so rewarding, however.*

understood that some streets had almost 90% shared homes. However, the ruling Liberal Democrats on the city council voted down the plan, arguing that shared housing was the only way many people could afford to live in Cambridge. Other university towns have suffered in the same way, and have begun to introduce licensing schemes in an effort to bring some orderliness to an unregulated situation.

There is another development spoiling the suburbs. People require more space. They may have to accommodate a grown-up son or daughter who cannot afford to move out – a trend on the increase in our overpriced housing market – or they may simply want another bedroom, a home office, a family room, a large lifestyle-statement kitchen. But finding the ideal modern detached home is difficult and expensive, beyond the means of many; house-price inflation has increased the size of the mortgage needed to take that step up. The alternative is to extend. Suburban gardens are generally quite long but narrow, and while a ground-floor extension can enlarge the kitchen, new bedrooms or offices often have to go into the roof. Some of these loft conversions are skilful. Many, in the typical inter-war semi, are not; they are simply boxes in the roof, ungainly and ugly. They distort the original rooflines and stare unpleasantly over neighbours' gardens. Where one once looked up from the kitchen or sitting room at a pitched roof, one now finds little eyes gazing back from dormer windows.

Suburbs are also sinking into a swamp of motor vehicles. In old photographs roads seem much wider, including the narrow streets of speculative housing off Mill Road. Most of Cambridge's houses went up before car ownership became general, and they lack garages. Today, when each household seems to possess at least two cars, front gardens disappear under gravel or tarmac, and grass verges are turned into rutted mud baths. In addition, once-wide roads are narrowed to a single lane by all-day commuter parking, especially anywhere within walking distance of the station, Addenbrooke's, the Science Park or the city centre. Even on newer estates where garages and perhaps double garages are provided, the disfigurement remains. Man's natural sloth inclines him to leave his car(s) on the drive rather than trouble to put them away, besides which many are nowadays too large and bulbous to fit into a garage of normal dimensions. Particularly deplorable is the phenomenon of keeping the company van at home. It is doubtless convenient for the worker and also for the company that need not have a depot for such vehicles, but the effect in the suburb is to blur the distinction between work and home, and to mar the view.

*The blight of loft conversion can range from oversized dormers (top) to complete portakabins seemingly dropped from the sky.*

As traffic congestion grows, some suburban roads are unlucky enough to become rat runs. Even getting out of one's own drive can be a protracted business. Crazed motorists are regularly confronted by 'traffic calming' measures that do not always have the intended effect. Already-desperate drivers risk their suspension and exhausts as they vault traffic humps at unwise speeds, then accelerate to the next hazard to make up lost time. This is unkind to the ears of residents and damaging to road surfaces. The more elaborate arrangements of bollards, humps and chicanes make roads more, not less, hazardous and are a godsend to boy racers who, as in Cherry Hinton High Street, time themselves through these exciting obstacles. And of course signs appear where no signs were, and suburbia is further urbanised. The photo at the top of the following page shows the result of well-meaning intervention in Radegund Road – messy and ugly, no matter how effective. A more sensitive approach can be seen beneath it, from a garden-suburb quarter of Odense in Denmark, where simple beech hedges narrow the road and no signs intrude.

*Exciting traffic calming measures on Cherry Hinton High Street.*

Further ugliness has been caused by tinkering with roundabouts. They used to be attractive islands of well-chosen planting, across which all potential hazards could be seen. But thanks to the habit of motorists approaching and entering them at high speed, it was thought necessary to make them more conspicuous by elevating them above a black and white chevron

*Green verges vanish as car ownership exceeds the available parking space.*

*Two styles of traffic calming - the English in Radegund Road (above) and the Danish on Langelinie, Odense (below).*

design that resembles old-fashioned public lavatory tiling. (Incidentally, it is unclear what proportion of drivers did not see roundabouts before this innovation and drove straight across them.) The planting of shrubs, even trees, rather than flowers on these raised islands now makes it impossible to see traffic entering the roundabout directly ahead, and therefore harder to make sensible calculations about when to join the roundabout oneself. This was no doubt intended to make motorists slow down and take more care; in fact it has made roundabouts more alarming and more dangerous, particularly for cyclists, whose acceleration from a standing start cannot match the speed of a car coming round the blind corner like the proverbial bat out of hell. At the time of writing, a cyclist is 'stable' in hospital with 'life-changing' injuries after colliding with a lorry at the Cherry Hinton Road/Mowbray Road roundabout. The wonder is that there have not been more such collisions. The most ludicrous aspect of this peculiar attempt at road safety is that small advertising boards are allowed on the islands. What are we meant to look at? Oncoming traffic hazards which we can barely see until the last second, or the signboard advertising 'Acme Car Crash Insurance'?

Suburbs are not entirely discrete areas of housing. They mingle with the premises of utilities and 'works', as the maps call them. If these become redundant, drastic redevelopment takes place. For example, following the closure of the Pye works, the area around Chesterton church was redeveloped on a giant scale. The church has been blotted out by towering

*The modern 'blind' roundabout - a potentially lethal hazard for all road users, and especially for cyclists.*

**161**

*Hampden Gardens, one of three mega-developments in Cromwell Road.*

apartment blocks in streets bearing predictably pretentious names – Scholars' Walk and Pepys Court among them – and in styles that could not jar more with the area's older buildings. Meanwhile Cromwell Road, where established semis are already faced by the massive barracks of Winstanley Court and Hampden Gardens, is experiencing its third mega-development in recent years, the bafflingly named Veritas. The volume of traffic generated by these new warrens is lamentable, and of course glibly disregarded by the developers. Rustat Road will have a similar expansion of its elephantine apartments when the former Cambridge Water Company site is developed. Anyone buying a house in the suburbs needs to look very carefully at the proximity of school playing fields, football grounds and small works: there is every likelihood of their being sold off for 'housing', for which read 'mega-mansions'.

Today there is no such thing as an 'established' suburb. While developers and buy-to-let landlords are making their profits, suburban amenity is being eroded. There is almost constant extending and infilling, demolition and rebuilding, and the incessant chugging of cement mixers augmented by the whine of electric saws. Pretentious stylistic gimmicks of 'contemporary living' produce buildings offensively unsuitable to the tone of the area. Trees and shrubs are lost, leaving horrid gaps like missing teeth. Familiar landmarks disappear, pubs are boarded up pending conversion to flats, commuter cars invade, large enclaves of anonymous apartment dwellers replace the neighbour over the garden hedge, and wheelie bins multiply. And ever present is an insidious anxiety, the fear of some new and intrusive development.

*Part of the vast Veritas site under construction.*

**8**

**The riverside**

A river is a compelling attraction, though not always picturesque. For centuries rivers were the chief means of transporting heavy goods. Workshops and warehouses clung to the banks by a town just as they later clustered like iron filings round the magnet of the railway.

Waterfronts can be a miracle of beauty, as in Venice. More often they can be a nightmare, as in London. The river at Cambridge has had mixed fortunes. If we follow it from the south we meet first the incomparable view across Grantchester Meadows, providentially preserved from relief roads and housing estates. The Fen Causeway controversially cut across it in 1926-7, and a very unpleasant university Engineering block, the Inglis Building, was dumped there at Coe Fen in 1945. But further on we encounter a delightful panorama of Peterhouse and its ancient wall, the Fitzwilliam Museum, the Pitt Building, the tower of the Emmanuel United Reformed Church and a wide expanse of 'fen' – that is, land prone to flood and therefore devoid of buildings. Indeed, from certain angles none can be seen at all, and in May with the blossom and cow parsley it is a wonderfully rural scene – and cows do still graze on 'Cow Fen'.

*Coe Fen, looking towards Peterhouse and the tower of Emmanuel United Reformed Church.*

As we near Silver Street Bridge there are picturesque buildings like the Old Granary to admire, but the former Garden House Hotel cannot be classed with them. One may note in passing that it is now styled the 'Doubletree by Hilton', an example of how local associations are being removed by global corporations determined to remake the world in their own bland image.

There has recently been an unsurprising controversy over plans to increase the size of the hotel to a catastrophic extent in this very sensitive area.

Enough damage has already been done by the University Centre or Grad Pad, built in 1967. This is quite in a class of its own. Once likened to a multistorey car park with windows, it also has more than a hint of the medieval fortress about it. If there had been a competition for the worst possible building to place on the site, this crass, brutal, insensitive structure would have romped home the winner.

Not to be outdone, Queens' did their best – or worst – on the other side of Silver Street bridge. Here, on the west bank of the river, every Queens' building is a mistake. The Fisher Buildings are dull, while Cripps and Lyon Courts could hardly be less appropriate for this important site. Their white-painted concrete catches and reflects sunlight to a degree that is almost painful to look at, a literal eyesore. It is deplorable that the Backs begin with these offensive structures. Perhaps one day they will be demolished and replaced by buildings that live up to their situation, but we are unlikely to see that in our time.

*Silver Street Bridge - on one side an almost unchanged pastoral scene, on the other Cripps Court, a dense clutter of brick, concrete and glass.*

The stretch we are now approaching was once the commercial centre of Cambridge before the coming of the colleges. What we see today, however, is largely the creation of the 18th century at its most civilised, and one of the wonders of the world. The Backs provide a rare visual experience; views of fine old buildings and perfect lawns seen across a placid river from an avenue thick with trees. It is a composition of remarkable felicity and we are fortunate to have it. It is also a place to be on foot. But what do we allow? A maelstrom of cars, coaches, vans and lorries, a perpetual noise, a continual distraction of life-threatening fast movement, a hideous clutter of ugly parked vehicles and disfiguring traffic signs and lights. In the 19th century there was even a lunatic proposal to site the railway station here. If we want an example of man's capacity to spoil a thing of beauty we need look no further than this.

Suppose there were no road along the Backs. Then suppose there were a proposal to build one. There would be outrage, just as there was when a road across Grantchester Meadows was suggested. Let us try closing the Backs to traffic for just one day of the year to see how agreeable it is and to recognise the folly of the present arrangements. Why should getting from A to B as fast as possible be the absolutely first and paramount consideration? Why not establish a different priority? There are plenty of roads. There is only one Backs. Why spoil it? Why not admit that Queens' Road is a bad mistake and close it?

*Eighteenth-century landscaping ruined by 21st-century traffic - the Backs and Queens' Road.*

*What the postcards don't show - the world-famous view of King's Chapel taken from the far side of Queens' Road.*

When the Holford Report of 1950 recommended restricting traffic along the Backs, only 280 vehicles a day passed through – one every three minutes. It also suggested a speed limit of 15 mph and hoped that new relief roads would draw off the through traffic and leave Queens' Road to local traffic. Well, we now have the A14 and the M11 to draw off through traffic but 'local' traffic, if that is what it is, has grown to take up the slack. If there is a road, it seems people will use it. It is now time to go further than Holford and say that even local traffic should not go there.

'But where will the traffic go?' people will say. One would like to think it wouldn't go at all; 'Is your journey really necessary?' With Cambridge on the verge of what the newspapers call 'gridlock', the situation is already hopeless, and the absence of one short road will surely make little difference. The problem was debated sixty years ago to no effect; it is clearly insoluble if one thinks only of managing traffic, which is simply tinkering with the symptoms while the cause remains untouched. Let us rather tackle a problem we can solve, that of restoring tranquillity to what the Holford Report called 'one of the world's most beautiful assemblies of buildings and grass and trees'.

As we continue downstream, we pass the Jerwood Library of Trinity Hall, Wren's Library at Trinity and the Bridge of Sighs at St Johns, before arriving at the stretch beyond Magdalene Bridge. Here, Quayside (1983) and Beaufort Place (1986) present a cleaner face to the river than did the old electricity works and its chimney, demolished in 1982. Magdalene College gardens grace the left bank before the view opens up once more with Jesus Green on the right. Opposite, on slightly higher ground, runs Chesterton Road. We are at least spared a view of terrace backsides here, as building only took place on the further side of the street. But among the 19th-century town houses, on the corner of Carlyle Road, squats the incongruous Henry Giles House. Originally built in 1959 for the now defunct Cambridge Instrument Company, this office block is currently occupied by the Department of Work and Pensions, and also houses the Cambridge Job Centre. The sight of its dull square bulk provokes the same reaction as if one came home to find a milk crate hurled into one's front garden.

*Henry Giles House on Victoria Road, originally built for the Cambridge Instrument Company and now the Cambridge Job Centre.*

Beyond Victoria Bridge, the left bank is enhanced by Boathouse Court (1989). This imaginative development of seven houses makes skilful use of a small footprint, its design referring loosely to neighbouring boathouses with their uncommon mixture of workshop utility and heraldic emblazoning. Midsummer Common stretches away on the right bank; Cambridge is extremely fortunate to have this medieval survival reaching in so far towards the centre. Building was historically confined to higher ground above the risk of floodwater, and on the ridge above can be seen the undistinguished houses and flats of Parsonage Street and Auckland Road. They must have a fine view, but it is not possible to return the compliment.

*Boathouse Court on Trafalgar Road, viewed from Midsummer Common.*

Further on is the former site of Cambridge Regional College, where new developments by Berkeley Homes are nearing completion. Cambridge Riverside is an extensive five-storey stretch of apartments commanding the low ridge above the river. The first part of this huge complex to be offered for sale was Marlowe House. Its name refers to Christopher Marlowe of Corpus Christi College, the Elizabethan playwright and government spy who was stabbed to death in a drunken tavern brawl; not, perhaps, the scholarly association the developers were hoping to conjure up amongst discerning buyers making what their newspaper adverts call 'an educated choice'. Unsurprisingly, Marlowe House offers luxury apartments for the well-to-do ('prices on application') though some might think that a one-bedroom flat, however well appointed, is hardly the height of opulence. The prices should at least keep out the drunken tavern brawlers, and the 'concierge service' (no vulgar 'porter' or 'caretaker' here) will be on the alert twenty-four hours a day. There is also an 'exclusive' gym should a stroll by the river fail to provide sufficient buttock toning.

*Cambridge Riverside - invasive over-development close to the Cam.*

The Cambridge Riverside buildings are every bit as intrusive as one feared they would be. They appear unsettlingly and confusingly above the roofline of the terrace of Victorian houses to the east, while seen from Victoria Avenue they push well down the slope of the water meadow and cut across the view. Close to, they dominate the river path with a multitude of balconies, terraces and floor-to-ceiling windows, displaying the intimidating scale one has come to expect from large redevelopments. The curved, jutting bays call to mind the futuristic tanks in Korda's film 'Things to Come'; one almost expects them to come rolling down the slope, guns blazing.

*The roofline of Cambridge Riverside peeps above the old terrace, unsettling this once-fine view of the river's gentle curve.*

Of course, not all buyers will want to take up residence in these 'luxuriously specified' flats with 'glorious views over the River Cam'. In a telling sentence the advert reads, 'whether you're buying as an investment, or living at Cambridge Riverside ...', and the word order is significant. This development is aimed at the *rentier* class before the householder. Houses and flats are no longer merely homes, they are investments. We have seen where that has led in recent years.

Beyond Elizabeth Way bridge we approach the fringes of the old industrial district of Cambridge, where brick pits, kilns, gas works and the like once disfigured the area to our right. The Victorian terrace houses of Riverside appear quaint and homely on account of their human scale, in marked contrast to what has been built further along.

Keeping our attention to the south side of the river we pass, on the corner of River Lane, a dull, heavy block of biscuit/orange brick called 'The Mallards', a development so nondescript that it almost works. While some new buildings along here try too hard, this one does not try at all. It could be a modern signal box scaled up. People live there.

Riverside Place, by contrast, strives to make an impact, and regrettably it succeeds. What should be a peaceful stretch of river, easing its way into the meadows, is treated to a piece of Docklands. It instantly brings to mind regenerated derelict quaysides in big cities, populated by overpaid young bankers. But this is the River Cam, not many yards from Stourbridge Common and Ditton Meadows. Riverside Place is simply too smart for its location. It is a good building in some respects. Seen from the Victorian terrace houses, it rises up attractively using a cleverly staggered roofline

*Metropolitan chic, in the form of Riverside Place, towers incongruously over trees, riverboat homes and the dowdy Mallards.*

*A relic of old Riverside - the former sewage pumping station, now the Museum of Technology.*

which respects the curve of the river. But it is too conspicuous in its glaring white and starkly contrasting black trim. The choice of black and white hints at chic minimalist living but also carries associations of old-fashioned tiled bathrooms and public lavatories. At the same time – and this almost goes without saying – it is too big and domineering. It intrudes metropolitan glitz into a near-pastoral scene.

Beyond it, next to the Museum of Technology, stands St Bartholomew's Court, a visually unsuccessful development of 92 properties (see photo overleaf). Once again, an important reason for this is its sheer bulk. Some attempt has been made to provide variety within an overall symmetry but the result is fussy and in no particular style. The two ends have Lutyens-like features but the main façade lacks the strength and clarity of Lutyens. It is cluttered with black metal balconies that are supported by central pillars unsettlingly like drainpipes. The red brick panels add to the confusion and – though no doubt intended to give relief to the yellow brickwork – are probably a mistake. This is merely the river frontage of a courtyard development of such size and density of population as to possess an unreal, distorted, almost nightmarish quality. There is nothing inviting about it.

171

Water View Apartments is a smaller and much more attractive building, perfectly modern and with no historic allusions. Approaching it from the west we are first aware of the buttress-like walls of yellow brick as it follows the curve of the river; brick walls are wonderfully calming quiet things. Its proportions are comfortable and the flats look inviting, though regrettably the balconies are white where the window frames are black and fashioned from crude metalwork, like a utilitarian railway bridge of the 19th century. Since the building faces north it is hard to see the need for the projecting light filters at the top, which resemble metal door mats or shoe scrapers. This is almost the only stylistic cliché that stands out on a pleasingly clean and simple design.

Riverside House in dull brown brick comes next. Visually it is a perfectly pointless building. Beyond it lies a short Victorian terrace – and what a

*The clumsy miscellany of styles and references that is St Bartholemew's Court.*

*Facing page*

*Top: Stourbridge House.*

*Bottom: Water View Apartments - successfully of its time and a handsome addition to the water front.*

relief to pass buildings that do not loom – before we reach Stourbridge House, a very cheap-looking 1960s-style block of flats. Saving on brick, the developers employed easily discoloured white timber and provided enormous white balconies, quite out of scale and looking like giant window boxes. The entire façade is of glass and white timber and could not glare out more rudely. Viewed from the east it looks like a chest of drawers left partly open. It originally had a flat roof, which increased the resemblance. As we leave it behind, Stourbridge Common opens up on the right, while ahead of us the river continues on towards Fen Ditton.

Let us now return to Elizabeth Way Bridge and consider the north side of the Cam. Right by the bridge stands the Eights Marina, a nicely composed group of apartments but strangely dull, possibly due to the colour of the brick. Like too many new gated developments along the river front, it snarls 'exclusive, strictly private, keep out'.

Beyond the bridge the bank is lined with trees as far as the stretch opposite Water View Apartments. At this point the willows thin out to reveal some phenomenally horrible-looking residences on the former site of the Pye works. The spire of St Andrew's Church, which should dominate this view towards Chesterton, is now miserably obscured. Four banal six-storey tower blocks stand in a meadow, each displaying the cliché of a top floor clad in wood in an attempt to disguise their height. Why bother? Their obligatory balconies are stuck on like fire escapes, no doubt a cheaper option than making them an integral part of the construction. The blocks do offer a kind of sculptural grouping, even if resembling a row of crates, but this small merit is negated by the catastrophic jostling jumble of new buildings behind. All kinds of awkward, messy, ugly, conflicting façades, planes and rooflines are visible through the gaps between the four blocks. The insensitivity that allowed this metropolitan rabbit warren to be dumped down in

*The view north towards Chesterton. The spire of St Andrew's Church is lost behind atrocious new flats parked on ancient water meadows.*

*Well-proportioned, low-impact housing on the north bank of the Cam at Fen Road.*

the heart of old Chesterton, directly facing the church, calls into question the eyesight of the planners. However, there is a good deal of unoccupied space between the blocks and the river, so in due course this repellent view might be hidden by something else – whether equally vile remains to be seen.

Further on, the north bank runs parallel to Water Street and then Fen Road. Along this stretch it is built up with fairly ordinary two-storey houses almost to the railway bridge. The gardens running down to the river are short, trees are few and the prospect is without distinction. The one cardinal merit is that the buildings are low and mostly unostentatious. But just before the railway bridge there is a very successful group of nine modern homes, low, compact, solid, and with splendidly proportioned roofs. The bedrooms, situated in these deep roofs, are lit by Velux windows, thereby avoiding the sort of staring first-floor fenestration that taller houses would present. This is an intelligent way to face the river. The woodwork is in dark stain which harmonises with the brick, but inevitably some recent alterations have been insensitive; one house has gone for glaring white patio doors, which is like wearing white socks with a dark suit. The soft grey slate of the roofs is weathering nicely with touches of lichen. These fine buildings show up the uninspiring range that lies next to the railway bridge.

The bridge itself could usefully be repainted a better colour. At present it suggests that odd lots of paint were used up on it. To the south, a dull estate of flat-roofed, white-fascia-boarded mediocrities mars the ridge, while beyond the railway bridge lies the still unspoilt vista of Fen Ditton church.

**175**

After this chapter was drafted, a significant row broke out in the press. 'Scruffy cars and boats are spoiling the view' ran the headline in the News and Crier on 22 December 2011. It was a telling example of the 'Them and Us' attitude of gated communities, since the area in question lies in front of St Bartholemew's Court. Residents there complained that the appearance of the riverside was a disgrace, spoilt by scruffy boats, poorly maintained railings and a bizarre collection of vehicles ranging from camper vans to 'Soviet-style vehicles' and 'old fire engines'. (I'd like to have seen those.) Clearly this was lowering the tone of the neighbourhood. Demands were made that there should be double yellow lines and residents' parking only.

*Local colour or local eyesore? One of the so-called 'Soviet-style' vehicles parked at Riverside.*

It is significant that this has only become an issue since the arrival of the new apartment blocks. The railings could certainly do with some fresh paint, but it seems considerable cheek to complain about the houseboat owners whose residence long precedes that of the apartment dwellers. The boats are part of the character of the area. One might more justifiably complain about the ghastly blocks of flats on the other side of the river. The stretch of road and its associated parking is no worse than anywhere else near the centre of Cambridge. While all this might be an honest complaint about an undesirable scruffiness outside smart new flats, it also implies a complaint about 'undesirable' people (who drive Soviet-style vehicles and can't afford luxury flats). Some might even think it amounts to an attempt at social cleansing. It could also lead to council action and considerable expense to the taxpayer; a sum of £400,000 was predicted to build pontoons and ladders for proper access between the boats and the bank. Boats are moored at Riverside without fee, unlike on other parts of the river, as nobody seems to own it. The council is now looking to register the embankment as being in its ownership (on what authority?) so that it can impose regulations. As we have seen earlier in the case of shopping malls, public space then becomes private property and subject to Big Brother-style conditions, a state of affairs as ugly in its own way as the untidiness that it tries to remove.

## 9

# The fringes

The city boundary lacks clean, well-defined edges; radiating roads take ribbon development out towards nearby villages, new housing begins to fill the spaces in between, university buildings spread westwards into the countryside and stand next to cultivated fields, as does Addenbrooke's to the south. But at the fringes, refreshing pockets of semi-wilderness remain, and it would be a very good thing to leave these untouched. While tidy parks and recreation grounds are all very well, to say nothing of the various closes, pieces and greens, they cannot have the same kind of appeal as those areas that show little trace of the hand of man, or at any rate the hand of the council.

This is particularly true of the fringes to the east, where commons remain and where old quarries have been abandoned. The flooded chalk pits of the former cement works have lain undisturbed for a quarter of a century, making them an ideal habitat for wildlife. In particular, that shyest of birds, the kingfisher, may be sighted along the adjacent brook running from Cherry Hinton to Coldhams Lane.

Mercifully, some sort of plan for a marina back in the 1980s was abandoned, as the water is dangerously deep. Kingfishers and motor boats are incompatible. Recreation need not entail noise, machines or special equipment, and it is a great blessing that the area has been left as tranquil as anywhere can be under an airport flight path.

*One of the flooded chalk pits on the eastern fringe of Cambridge - a natural haven for wildlife.*

However, when this book was almost finished, the city council published its new Cambridge Local Plan, which contained the ominously titled chapter 'Opportunity Areas'. This describes the area south of Coldhams Lane as 'a potential "green and blue corridor"' that could be opened up for recreational use, including cycling, five-a-side football and the creation of a BMX track. In fact there is nothing potential about this 'corridor' – it is already there, but left to nature. What is actually meant is that there is potential for spoiling it. The report does acknowledge the need 'to take into account the nature conservation value of these sites', but so might Brazilian loggers speak of the Amazon rainforest. Once an area is 'exploited' for whatever purpose it is lost to any realistic nature conservation. As soon as this plan was published the local paper reported talk of creating a 'Romsey Beach', along with water sports and all the rest of it. In the letters that followed there was little or no mention of wildlife, the dangerous depth of the quarries, the inevitable 'landscaping' and tidying up, the influx of cars and car parks, signage or any other facilities that regulations might require. This is an area which has long felt like the edge of Cambridge, the place where Mill Road peters out, where a mile of open space separates the city from Cherry Hinton. Man does not have to crash around and poke into every corner, bringing his car and his rubbish with him. Why not leave it alone?

There is an ever-present threat of meddling and tidying, of despoiling or outright exploitation. It was a depressing experience some years ago to see notice boards and picnic benches appear at the Beechwoods beyond Wort's Causeway. The benches have now gone but new information boards have appeared – one actually inside the wood – and a scarlet bin for dog waste has also proved necessary. A former wooden gate has been blocked and the new galvanized steel entrance has an unpleasantly industrial character. Such additions are intended to be helpful to visitors, yet they are urban intrusions; they erode the very qualities of the woodland that people seek when going there. A wood needs no explanation. Those who value such places do not need explanatory signs, and those who do not – who want to vandalise, chuck cans, torch stolen cars or leave old mattresses and builder's rubble – will not bother to read them; they are far more likely to deface them. The signage is no doubt well-intentioned, but then so are warnings on packets of nuts saying 'may contain nuts'.

Over-zealous tidying and planting has pointlessly tamed the little group of trees at Burnside. The undergrowth was cut down and the ground rotovated – do bluebell woods get rotovated? – before box and laurel were planted. These are

*Signs for the inattentive at the Beechwoods, Wort's Causeway.*

*Only the street furniture and tidied-up undergrowth indicate suburbia at Burnside.*

*The signboard at Snakey Path.*

not natural undergrowth plants and they are struggling, quite apart from looking wrong. This place should have been more or less left alone, not turned into a Victorian shrubbery. And at nearby Snakey Path a signboard has appeared, giving information about the local wildlife. The regrettable result is to destroy any sense of mystery about this green avenue and where it might lead. Signboards have also appeared in Cherry Hinton Hall Park, among them one announcing a 'Children's Natural Play Area' – which, far from being natural, contains all manner of man-made climbing and swinging furniture, and benches for the parents. People should read Jerome K. Jerome's comments on the German love of order and the taming of a picturesque mountain torrent ('Three Men on the Bummel', Chapter VII) before thinking of tidying up. Otherwise we shall have what Jerome feared, 'a seat every fifty yards, a police notice every hundred, and a restaurant every half-mile'.

Coldham's Common has some very satisfactory untidy bits around its edges, the sort of places where children can imagine they are exploring jungles, or climbing Everest on the grassy mountain of chalk piled up in one corner. The view from the top of this mound, particularly in spring, is a rewarding sea of green. Only the inevitable dull roar of traffic from Barnwell Road intrudes on the Common's semi-rural tranquility.

*Paradise lost.*

Of course, getting from A to B in the shortest time by car is always paramount with planners, and it is unlikely that we have heard the last of the scheme to run a 'relief' road through the Common. The Newmarket railway already runs along near the western edge, but is happily screened by trees, and the trains are very infrequent; on a road there is no such thing as infrequent traffic. Incredibly, there was once even a plan to build a motor racing circuit here.

The northwestern edge of the Common by Coldhams Lane bridge merges into one of those half-neglected 'edgelands' by the railway line (see photo at the top of p. 185). Such places have their own curious attraction, being almost abandoned yet retaining traces of a former use. Though unlovely, they have a charm similar to unfrequented overgrown ancient ruins with their absence of people and their air of being overlooked and forgotten. They contain items of miscellaneous junk to enthuse 'sculptors' of 'found objects', and 'weeds' and wild flowers that have escaped the poisons of modern farming. They are places where one hopes the sign affixers, the chainsaw wielders, the rotovators, the improvers and the obsessive compulsive tidiers will be kept well out of harm's way. It is in just such corners that shy wildlife can flourish unmolested and unexterminated.

*This field, between traffic-choked Barnwell Road and Coldham's Lane, exemplifies the unexpected delights of the fringes.*

The wide belt of trees dividing the Common from Barnwell Road is dense enough to give the illusion of escape from suburbia, while the view from there to Coldhams Lane (pictured on p. 181) could be miles into the country-side. On the east side of Barnwell road is another miracle of preservation, Barnwell Nature Reserve. It was formerly a piggery, set in an area where the beasts could forage, and a few overgrown blocks of concrete remain. When Barnwell Road was built in 1974 it was supposed that industrial units would soon line the east side. This has not happened, and the area of chalk scrub has been left with two signboards, some fencing around the pond and relatively discreet management to prevent the place becoming wholly overgrown.

Limekiln Close, the old chalk workings at Cherry Hinton opposite the Robin Hood pub, is another good example of a relative wilderness. It too is managed to a certain extent, but not manicured. Grown up with trees since it was abandoned as a clunch quarry at the end of the 19th century, it is like a lost world. To a child's mind, or to an adult mind that retains an imagination, this could be Conan Doyle's lost valley in miniature, or a tropical jungle where anything might be encountered. There are no deliberate vistas, no tarmac, just a tangle of vegetation inviting exploration.

*Limekiln Close Nature Reserve resembles the entrance to a magical realm.*

*Three visitors dwarfed by the massive amphitheatre of Cherry Hinton's East Pit Nature Reserve.*

Adjacent to it is the East Pit, which until the 1980s was a working quarry. It has information boards, a dog waste bin, a couple of surfaced paths and metal staircases up the steeper pitches, but the site is large enough to absorb these. This vast amphitheatre – reminiscent of the volcanic crater Solfatara in the Bay of Naples – could swallow up the Colosseum or Wembley Stadium with ease. Once inside it, you are entirely secluded from the outside world and the madness of traffic on the Cherry Hinton-Fulbourn road. Fortunately, on account of its rare chalkland plants it has been declared a Site of Special Scientific Interest, rather than a new home for Cambridge United or a motor cycle scramble venue. (Hands up those who like the whine of revving Hondas.) It is good to know that the authorities occasionally recognise the value of recreation that does not involve protracted loud noises. One hopes that Lime Kiln Road, the narrow lane outside with its high hedges, will never be widened. It is something of a rat run, but there is no need to encourage this.

Close by, facing the Robin Hood pub, lies the tree-fringed hollow and pool known as Giant's Grave, whose springs were the original source of water for Cherry Hinton. Past the inevitable information board one enters a different world, out of time. On a windless, heavy grey October day with pale yellow leaves floating on the water, one might almost expect to see the

Lady of Shallott, as depicted by J.M. Waterhouse, drifting by. And the springs here have much older resonances, of a place venerated by pre-Christian peoples, who often made such locations the focus of religious rituals. Although re-landscaped when the road junction was widened in the 1960s, it is not over-manicured and retains a good deal of its ancient magic.

Another eastern edgeland runs between Cambridge and Fen Ditton, where a narrow strip interrupts the ribbon development along Ditton Lane, and separates the village from the suburb. It is the line of the old Mildenhall Railway, whose rails were taken up fifty years ago. A cycleway now follows it for some distance before turning into the Newmarket Road Park and Ride (which incidentally is very well laid out and screened). Can we hope that this green buffer will remain in years to come, or is Fen Ditton also doomed to become a suburb of Cambridge?

To the north and west, the edge of the city is effectively bounded by the A14 and M11. New development is spreading up to these roads like a child filling in the white spaces of a colouring book. If only we could be sure that these dismal boundaries will remain as the city limit. But one might predict that it is only a matter of time before reasons will be found to build on the far side of them – in these incontinent times the temptation will be too great.

*Industrial landscape and countryside intermingle by Coldham's Lane railway bridge...*

*...while just a few yards away, cattle graze on Coldham's Common.*

**185**

The city's southern edge is now being compromised. The belt of trees on the south side of Long Road once marked the beginning of open country. Now it partly screens the vast development which is being built at Clay Farm ('Great Kneighton'). Already a large access road has chopped its way through; for a hundred yards or more the tree belt on either side of the junction has been cut back to half its depth to create sight lines for the traffic that will soon teem in and out, and a wider road, traffic lights and pedestrian railings now stand where trees and tangled undergrowth once thrived.

Allotments deserve a mention in this chapter. They can hardly be described as wildernesses but they are green areas, not bricks and mortar, and they provide welcome open spaces of a highly individual kind. There is something satisfying about them. They are mildly subversive in a stubborn, passive way, with allotment holders escaping the pressures of modern life for a few hours and defying Health and Safety diktats in their ramshackle sheds made of corrugated iron and old doors. The very existence of allotments is a splendid fist-shake in the faces of developers who would love to concrete them over. Long may they last.

# 10

# Vistas

In landscaped gardens vistas are calculated. In urban landscapes they are more often accidental; a new building may be designed to complement its neighbours, but the wider effect, even of tall buildings, is not always precisely calculated.

St John's Chapel is a good example. When it was finished in 1869, critics deplored its size as being wholly out of proportion to the First Court, and they regretted the destruction of a proper quadrangular enclosure. On the other hand, the tower inadvertently provided an attractive focal object from several vantage points. The view from Portugal Place (shown left) can hardly have been contrived, but what a fortunate accident. The tower similarly contributes to the town landscape seen through Rose Crescent or from Chesterton Road, to give but two more examples.

The other tall building that brings similar accidental benefits is the Catholic Church. It was not placed where it is just to enhance the gardens of Downing College or the view across Parker's Piece, yet that is exactly what it does. As the tallest building in Cambridge it also lends interest to the distant prospect, particularly as it is a spire and not a glass and concrete tower block.

Unsurprisingly, more recent buildings have compromised these views. Not long ago St John's tower was the only focal point when looking from Jesus Green towards Park Parade. But now there is a singularly undistinguished competitor on the skyline in the shape of the Varsity Hotel and Spa – and what a shape: an ungainly, squat seven-storey block in that all too common biscuit-coloured brick with a grey top. It rises unwelcome not only above its immediate neighbours but also over Park Parade and Jesus Green – indeed it is vexingly visible from a good many other places, for instance from the castle mound. What is especially annoying is that this is no accident. The

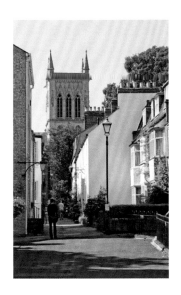

*Above: St John's tower from Portugal Place.*

*Right: The view from Jesus Green towards Park Parade, now marred by the Varsity Hotel and Spa.*

*Ineffectually camouflaged by grey cladding, the top storeys of the Varsity Hotel and Spa violate the privacy of local residents. The roof garden is particularly odious.*

architects must have known exactly what the impact would be because they have tried to soften it with the familiar trick of using lighter-coloured materials and more glass for the top two storeys. Their clients presumably cared not at all, as long as the design satisfied the planners. Maximum floor space and maximum revenue were their likely goals, and the Cambridge skyline could go hang.

Quite possibly the worst example of a vista spoiled is that at Parker's Piece. There are several buildings whose demolition would be an act of mercy and a public benefit, but near the top of the list has to be the extension to the Cambridge Local Examinations Syndicate, which faces the Catholic Church. It is a utilitarian block of shocking ugliness, and to see it across Parker's Piece next to the church spire is enraging. It is equally repugnant viewed from Lensfield Road. Everything about it is wrong – height, materials, design, location. It does not even show respect for the brick building to which it connects, and it utterly spoils the composition of trees, lawn and spire. Short of demolition, the only hope is that the younger trees along Gonville Place will eventually grow tall enough to conceal it. One might have hoped that such a glaring mistake would never be repeated. Not so.

*Viewed from the Portugal Street and the castle mound, the Varsity Hotel and Spa towers incongruously over the surrounding rooftops.*

*The disastrous Examinations Syndicate block by Parker's Piece.*

*Gargantuan Parkside Place dwarfs the neighbouring trees, formerly - and more fittingly - the tallest features of Parker's Piece.*

Parker's Piece has been further compromised by Parkside Place, another tall and unsuitable structure, this time at the southeast corner where the old fire station used to be. The artist's impression of this new development by Grosvenor made one's heart sink, and the reality confirms one's worst fears. Its tower rises offensively and inappropriately for eight storeys, well above the height of Parkside's mature trees, and calling it a 'landmark' building or a 'sustainable development' does nothing to improve it. A gas holder is a landmark building, as are Addenbrooke's incinerator chimneys; they are not triumphs of architecture. Parker's Piece does not need the looming presence of this cheese-grater tower with its huge staring windows. The spire of the Catholic Church works quite differently. It is attenuated, it has no windows to indicate human presence, it points to the heavens, it is a spiritual symbol. What kind of symbol is a block of luxury apartments?

Botanic House, by Station Road, also shows how catastrophically a tall building can affect its surroundings. However smart it may seem (to some), it contrives to cause damage all round. One of the glories of the Botanic Garden was that not a single building could be seen above its perimeter of trees. Standing barely half a mile from the city centre and the railway station one could be entirely unaware of the urban environment of bricks, glass and

*The seclusion of the Botanic Garden gatecrashed by Botanic House.*

concrete, shops and shoppers, trains and commuters. Only traffic noise intruded upon this vast and magnificent garden – until now. Botanic House's top three storeys of glaring windows make their impertinent appearance above and through the leafless trees in the same way that Millbank Tower inflicts itself upon Kensington Gardens. Who voted for that?

Then consider the view approaching either way along Hills Road. At one time the Catholic Church drew the eye, but Botanic House is so aligned as to barge its way across the vista like a roadblock, ruining any sense of perspective. From the railway bridge it presents a ghastly backdrop to the only building of merit in the area, the Royal Albert almshouses. Its enormous windows introduce a different and confusing scale, as well as a vile metro glitz quite at variance with the trees of the Botanic Garden and the quiet charm of the almshouses.

Like all tall buildings, Botanic House is visible from quite unexpected quarters, and it changes the aspect of more than just its immediate surroundings. From half a mile away in Mill Road one can turn into Mawson Road and be startled by the unwelcome sight of this glass tower.

*The view down Mawson Road from Mill Road. Is there any place from which Botanic House is not visible?*

*Botanic House shoulders its way across the street line at Hills Road.*

Other developments have created unseemly, even ludicrous, views and juxtapositions. Go to Park Street, look up Round Church Street and see the hideous contrast between the multistorey car park and St John's Chapel tower. Or stand on Jesus Green and look towards Chesterton Road to see whether the view is in any way enhanced by Henry Giles House. These are such unpleasant clashes of idiom that one can only suppose planners once envisaged the wholesale demolition and rebuilding of Cambridge in Brave New World styles.

*Round Church Street, where the multistorey car park brutalises a potentially fine view.*

Shops and offices inexorably rise ever higher until their heads pop up in unexpected places. The redeveloped row of shops in Regent Street, by Downing College, was built some thirty years ago to a height of four storeys, not only surpassing the original roofline and dominating the neighbours, but also showing its bulk above the buildings opposite and confusing the skyline seen from Parker's Piece. Tall shops have similarly affected Christ's College, which seems more lost than ever beneath the new and bigger Bradwell's Court. This latest version, known as 'Christ's Lane Cambridge', is better than the old, with good materials and an interestingly staggered façade (see photo overleaf). But it is bulky, and it lacks the human scale of its predecessor whose inner court gave such a pleasant sense of enclosure. Its roofline, moreover, is elevated by no fewer than fifteen luxury apartments which, despite being set back, are still undesirably visible from the street.

*The Christ's Lane development, with its fenestration and high-quality materials, partly acknowledges the neighbouring college buildings while overwhelming them with its height and scale.*

The reopening of Christ's Lane has exposed the dullest side of the college, although the proposed new library, if built, could well change the aspect of the lane for the better. And in a rare case of a new development actually creating a vista, the lane's reinstatement as a public thoroughfare has restored the view of Christ's Pieces from St Andrew's Street after a hiatus of over fifty years.

*Two views of the recently re-opened Christ's Lane, looking northeast at a view of the Pieces not seen in over a generation (left), and southwest towards St Andrew's Street (right).*

In Bridge Street, where late-medieval buildings were spared demolition in the 1930s, the banal, boxy elevation of the CATS College block (1987) was permitted to rise up behind them, wrecking another attractive roofline. Mackenzie Road suffered a different fate, as shown in the photo on the facing page. Here, the Victorian houses in the foreground draw the eye along a line of perspective that creates the expectation of a focal point far better than the one provided by the five-storey cliff of ARU's Coslett Building. This awful visual intrusion dates from the early 1970s, when such insensitivity was common; the construction and positioning of Botanic House suggests that nothing has been learnt in the four decades since.

*The huge cliff of ARU's Coslett Building crashes across the perspective of Mackenzie Road.*

*At the corner of Bridge Street and Round Church Street, a survival of old Cambridge has had its roofline wrecked by the CATS College block behind it.*

New vistas are being opened up around the railway station as part of the cb1 project. A road now runs from the station forecourt to Hills Road and Brooklands Avenue, and the prospect it offers, looking west, is appalling. Some of the nastiest buildings in Cambridge are exposed to view: the Cambridge Leisure multistorey car park, about as ugly as such a thing can be; the Belvedere; the bunker-like signal box, and the heavy, dark-brick jumble of the City House offices. The eye turns in vain to find a single thing of beauty to rest upon. And this, incredibly, is what visitors to Cambridge are presented with upon arrival by train.

The six-storey ARU student accommodation range attached to Foster's Mill runs the length of Station Place in an unbroken line. It has the all-too-common feature of a grey-clad top storey designed to conceal a building's true height – something that reeks of deviousness and sharp practice; seeing it on a daily basis makes one feel continually conned. Why Foster's Mill was allowed to remain is a mystery. Aesthetically it is a structure of no merit whatsoever and were it proposed today it would be – at least one hopes – firmly turned down. There is no point in keeping endless bits of redundant

*Station Place. This appalling windswept desolation is the visitor's first impression of Cambridge.*

*Facing page*

*Top: Foster's Mill after the fire.*

*Bottom: The mill's industrial bleakness is now repeated on a vast and depressing scale.*

industrial architecture unless they are of exceptional quality; photograph them and pull them down. One suspects that the mill was only spared in order to justify a roofline, allowing blocks to be built to the same height. Once it had served that purpose, a fire very nearly removed it to make way for more new buildings. While the resulting damage may have proved a blessing in disguise for the developer, it is nonetheless a pity that it rendered impractical the plan to turn part of the mill into a community centre.

Distant prospects of Cambridge are inevitably disturbed by the taller buildings now being permitted. The Marque and the Belvedere Dalek are obvious enough, but equally disturbing are other slightly lower but ungainly and oversized structures, especially the white-topped blocks of The Triangle, the apartments on Rustat Avenue and the Microsoft Building in

Station Road. Amongst other places, these can be seen from: Wandlebury; Chapel Hill above Haslingfield; the vantage point opposite the Roman road above Wort's Causeway, and even from several slightly elevated points along the Kingston-Eversden road some six miles away. At such a distance, nothing should be so conspicuous. Even Ely Cathedral does not stand out so, except when the sun shines on its lead roofs.

A church tower or spire is a suitable landmark for a distant city. Glaring white box tops like giant cereal packets are outrageously out of place. One sensibly proportioned human view after another is being spoilt by these unimaginative structures. A proper sense of hierarchy has the town hall and the church as the most important and therefore the tallest buildings. Today their significance is challenged by mediocre apartment blocks and offices, and the skyline starts to become a confusing jumble. Such is the march of progress.

*Seen from Lime Kiln Hill, to the east of Cambridge, the dominant features of the city skyline are of very recent construction.*

*Top, left to right: Cambridge Leisure Park, Botanic House, the re-clad Chemistry Building with Station Place beneath it, and the Microsoft Building.*

*Bottom, left to right: the Microsoft Building, the Triangle, the white-topped flats and red-clad apartment blocks on Rustat Avenue, and Parkside Place.*

## 11

# Motor traffic

Motor traffic has been mentioned in almost every single chapter so far and unavoidably so; it is one of the biggest causes of ugliness in our environment.

Firstly there is the noise, inescapable even in one's own home. And is there any outdoor place in Cambridge, or in 'remote' countryside for that matter, where the sound of motor vehicles does not penetrate? The unfortunates living in Orchard Park have a wall up against the noise from the A14, a desperate measure which is about as effective as trying to stop a tsunami with a stick. In our perverse world it takes a heavy snowfall to bring any knowledge of what a world without traffic might sound like.

Then there are the fumes. Thanks to catalytic converters they do not smell as bad as they did, but the fact remains that the combustion of petrol still turns fresh air into unhealthy if not actively poisonous substances. Diesel fuel emissions are much more noxious and dangerous. A recent study at the Massachusetts Institute of Technology concluded that each year about 5,000 people in Britain die prematurely from lung and heart diseases attributable to exhaust emissions; more than twice the number who are killed in road accidents.

*Not a car showroom but a filling station on a Saturday morning.*

Less obvious is the amount of oxygen removed from the atmosphere – a car will burn up almost fifty times as much as a cyclist in covering the same distance. And while not wishing to upset the fastidious, one might suggest noticing the colour of a handkerchief after use during a day spent in the heavily polluted streets of London. That blackness represents what your nose managed to exclude; smaller particles bury themselves in the lungs. Some Cambridge streets are scarcely less polluted.

Then, of course, there is the car's visual impact. Many current models are surprisingly ugly. In tune with the times they are often obese, and few are remotely desirable. Today even the Mini has a thick waist. Particularly embarrassing are 4x4 jeeps and vehicles like minibuses – vans with windows. The visual assault of traffic is further augmented by the extensive clutter of street furniture that is required to 'manage' it. Some reference to this has already been made in Chapter 3, but it needs to be emphasised that the accumulation of this material over the years has been extraordinary, and

*A sign in Great Eastern Street, Romsey, where cars now occupy space once reserved for pedestrians.*

*The one-way system in St Philip's Road, Romsey, requires absurd quantities of signage.*

*Mill Road, early on a midsummer morning, looks almost surreal without its usual river of traffic.*

visually very harmful. A quick look into any book of old photos of Cambridge makes the point. A hundred years ago there was almost no signage. Even fifty years ago there was relatively little. Today there are traffic signs galore – keep out, go slow, turn left, turn right, don't turn at all, don't stop, look out, *ad infinitum*. There are traffic lights, skyscraper street lights, vast electric signs showing the availability of parking, roundabouts, pedestrian crossings, subways, bollards, fences, rising bollards, kerbstones, speed humps and paint all over the roads. There are even traffic lights on roundabouts, a wonderful piece of Alice-in-Wonderland surrealism. And all of this is apparently necessary to prevent motorists from killing pedestrians or each other.

The roads themselves should not be forgotten. Roads are widened, new roads are proposed or made, and everything is done to keep the machines moving. The wider the road, the uglier it is; the scale becomes inhuman, hostile to pedestrians, and the other side becomes an unattainable distant shore. Huge signs stand up for the convenience of motorists, the information repeated two or three times to give them the chance to read it (they cannot be expected to slow down). Conversation on the street becomes difficult, if not impossible, on account of the racket of engine noise and the curious roar of fat tyres on tarmac. In narrower streets, the sound rebounds off the enclosing walls, and the fumes build up and linger. Is this a remotely sensible environment?

When it comes to managing traffic, planners seem to lose all sense of proportion. Cambridge has had its share of road 'improvement' schemes over the years, but some that were put forward – and thankfully never undertaken – were simply deluded. Even William Holford, whose planning suggestions for Cambridge in 1950 generally showed sense, took leave of his senses when it came to roads. It is a significant indication of his priorities that his report began with road proposals. He was rightly concerned to keep through traffic out of the centre – the congestion in 1950 is well shown in the report's photographs – and some of his ring road proposals eventually came to pass, notably the construction of Barnwell Road. But mercifully his main proposal, the Spine Relief Road, was not adopted. It was intended to take north-south traffic away from Magdalene Bridge, the Backs and the city centre, but at a huge environmental cost.

The road would have begun at a large roundabout on the junction of Histon Road, Huntingdon Road and Victoria Road. From there it would have run between Shire Hall and the gardens of Magrath Avenue to another large roundabout at Chesterton Road, involving the demolition of half a dozen houses. It was then to have bridged the Cam to emerge in a dual carriageway along Park Parade, eating up a strip of Jesus Green. Breaking through the charming row of cottages in Lower Park Street, it would have gone on to cross the middle of Jesus College's westernmost sports pitch on its way to Jesus Lane – demolishing Marshall's Garage for good measure.

*Park Parade, looking southeast towards Lower Park Street. In Holford's scheme, a dual carriageway would have run along here, demolishing the terrace ahead.*

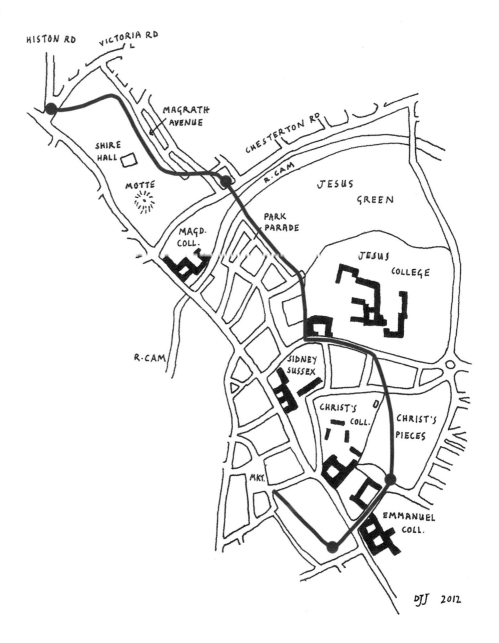

*The route of Holford's Spine Relief Road, proposed in 1950.*

At this point, aiming for Drummer Street, one alternative was to carry straight on through the gardens of Sidney Sussex and Christ's. The preferred alternative was to deflect east along Jesus Lane before turning south at Manor Street. In doing so, however, the road would not have followed the street line but would instead have taken out the houses on the corner and followed a line diagonally away – breaking through into King Street and out the other side – before performing its most spectacular piece of vandalism in cutting across Christ's Pieces. You couldn't make it up, as they say.

This scheme would have entailed the loss of two of the ten acres of Christ's Pieces, one and a half acres of Jesus Green, the Jesus College hockey pitch and a corner of Christ's Fellows' Garden. Holford apologetically wrote, 'We fully appreciate that Jesus College will hear of this proposal with regret... it being the one college to have escaped traffic annoyance thus far'. But, with an interesting inversion of priorities, he also commented ruefully on the position of Christ's Fellows' Garden: 'With that fatality which sometimes seems to attend road improvers, its Renaissance swimming bath and summer house are at the extreme northern end, and would thus be severed from the College if a road at ground level were taken through the garden.' Very inconsiderate of those early dons for having put those facilities there in the first place.

*These houses on the corner of Jesus Lane and Manor Street stand where Holford's Spine Relief Road would have driven its way through to Christ's Pieces.*

*Grantchester Meadows (top), Coe Fen (centre) and Coldham's Common (bottom), all menaced by traffic relief road schemes in former times, and thankfully preserved for us to enjoy today.*

Holford acknowledged that his plan involved drastic steps, but argued that without them the traffic congestion in the centre would soon become 'intolerable'. He certainly went into the problem carefully, explained the merits of alternative solutions, and looked to minimise construction costs and demolitions. Yet for all this, his basic premise was wrong, namely that motor vehicles must be accommodated. The best proof of the falsity of his position is that his Spine proposal was *not* carried out, that pedestrianisation of the centre was adopted instead, and in consequence we still have Christ's Pieces and Jesus still has its hockey pitch. The cure would have been worse than the disease, and we may be thankful that we have also been spared roads across Grantchester Meadows, Coe Fen and Coldham's Common.

In fact it has been apparent for many years now that attempts to accommodate motor traffic by road building are futile. A Parkinson's Law operates whereby car numbers expand to fill the space available to them. More roads equal more traffic. If, on the other hand, roads are closed for repairs, people cope and adapt as they did when the city centre was largely pedestrianised. True, the problem of congestion remains elsewhere, but we must consider our priorities. Do we want an end to traffic-choked shopping centres, noise and menace? Do we want hazardous rat runs to be closed off? And do we want to see streets cleared of signs, bollards and pedestrian barriers? Or do we want to assert the right of motorists to go wherever they please?

In recent decades Cambridge has moved towards creating priority for pedestrians and cyclists in the city centre, but there is still a long way to go. It is worth considering the results of experiments elsewhere. Copenhagen began in 1952 when car ownership in the city was barely 30% (even now it is less than 50%); Strøget, the mile-long main shopping street, was pedestrianised as long ago as 1962. Despite the fears of shopkeepers, the change was a great success, and footfall increased following the removal of cars. Copenhagen has also taken radical steps to encourage cycling, with similarly spectacular results; in the decade between 1995 and 2005 bicycle use increased by 50%. Road layouts have been made cycle friendly: at junctions a separate green light gives cyclists a six-second start to get safely on their way before cars are allowed to move. Motorists are extremely good at complying with these rules. Also, lights at pedestrian crossings now display numbers to count down the seconds you either have to wait, or have remaining to cross, reducing both the irritation of waiting and the possibility of becoming stranded if unwittingly setting out near the end of a green light sequence. On wider streets this is an invaluable safety feature.

Although Cambridge has also done much for cyclists, with some 22% of journeys in and around the city now taken by bike, we are still some way behind the enlightened Danes.

More could be done in Cambridge if we dared to reconsider our priorities. Car use too easily becomes Pavlovian to the point of addiction. There are perfectly fit and healthy people who probably never leave the house except in a car. Yet habits can be discouraged, even broken. Not so long ago it would have seemed impossible to rid enclosed public places and public transport of tobacco smoke, yet it has been done; smokers are now cast as luckless losers, condemned to get their fix in chilly corners outside their workplaces. It may yet be that the motorist will eventually gain pariah status too, at least when it comes to moving about city centres. When Lensfield Road is full of stationary traffic at 3 o'clock on a Friday afternoon, we have a state of affairs that is clearly stupid.

If motor traffic could be kept out of the central triangle altogether then the awful disfigurements of street furniture could be removed. Traffic lights and pedestrian crossings would not be needed, nor road paint, nor even the kerbs to pavements which give wheelchair users such a hard time. And perhaps the necessary delivery lorries could be restricted in size, thereby avoiding further damage to chipped corner buildings such as Whewell's Court.

That said, a traffic-free centre with no accompanying change in the cult of the car would simply transfer congestion elsewhere; one would have a pleasant, safer city centre, but the problem of what happens outside that charmed circle would remain. So while there is encouraging use of the Park and Ride system, its very success creates traffic nuisance elsewhere. There are current proposals to enlarge the Babraham Road parking site by up to 50%, but they are being contemplated with reluctance. It is in the Green Belt, and part of the very panorama the Cambridge Preservation Society protected with its Save the Gogs campaign in the 1930s.

Again one comes back to the fundamental problem of the car cult. Its votaries simply cannot imagine life without their machines. Putting an end to that would require a change of attitude beyond the power of any legislation. Look at the city's roads outside the supposed rush hours of morning and evening; they are still teeming with vehicles. Take note of the occupants and one sees that roughly half of them do not appear to be going about any

*Marooned - pedestrians on an island in a metal sea at Cambridge's Hyde Park Corner.*

very necessary errand – that is, they are not business people, deliverymen, taxi drivers or the emergency services. So what are they doing? Neither concerns about global warming, pollution nor the price of fuel seem to make any difference. 'Have car will travel'.

Yet the position is not entirely hopeless. It is possible to mitigate the impact of the car even outside the centre, and that is through the policy of 'Home Zones' or shared space. It is an idea pioneered by a quiet but persistent Dutch traffic engineer, Hans Monderman, who wondered whether street furniture gave motorists a false sense of security and stopped them using their eyes and common sense. Following the road deaths of two children in the village of Oudehaske in 1982, Monderman experimented with removing *all* street furniture. It worked even better than he had expected. He found that drivers cut their speeds by an average of 40% when driving through the village. The scheme has since spread to many other countries, including Britain, although British law, unlike Dutch law, has yet to establish legal priority for pedestrians and cyclists in such shared spaces. The idea of safety based on eye contact, common sense and reduced speeds is welcome not only in itself, but also as a means of vastly improving the appearance of towns.

A final point concerns the state of the roads themselves, whose surfaces are both ugly and uncomfortable. This is not just a result of cold winters or damage caused by drought. Many roads have ancient repairs that have sunk, or were made too proud in the first place and remain like railway sleepers. They can be felt even in a car, while the cyclist often has the sensation of riding a bucking bronco. Most of us have tales to tell of roads completely renewed that have been immediately drilled up by utility companies and 'made good' in a manner that negates the renewal. Even when not clumsily repaired, surfaces are often 'puddled', as though a herd of elephants had been let loose just before the tarmac hardened; one suspects a substructure of uneven rubble. Moreover, a surprising number of roads are easily flooded at the sides, either because the slope of the gutters fails to send the water into the drains, or because the drains themselves are clogged with leaves.

Of course, the council can allocate only so much money for roads, and as traffic grows so does the cost of highway maintenance. But once again it is instructive to look across the North Sea. In more than twenty years of cycle touring all over Denmark I have been struck by the superlative condition of their roads. Only in Copenhagen and in one or two towns have I ever been troubled by botched repairs of the railway-sleeper kind, and that infrequently. Irregularities like 'puddling' I have never seen; roads are consistently smooth and level. Even where a cycleway needs to cross a kerb, the ramp is perfectly calculated so that no jolting occurs – try to find that anywhere in Cambridge. It may be argued that the Danes, with a population of just five million, give their roads far less of a hammering, but the corollary is that there are far fewer taxpayers to maintain them. Yet still they build roads of a standard one can only dream of here. How do they do it? High taxes, no doubt, but also high standards of workmanship. It might be useful for our council to inquire further – as long as it doesn't involve a fact-finding mission over there at local taxpayers' expense.

# 12

# Things to come: the railway area

'The Station Road/Hills Road area has become a developer's dream…'

A developer's dream it might well be to Bob Ensch, area director of building contractors Morgan Sindall (reported in the News and Crier 26 May 2011), but to Cambridge residents the railway area is more like a nightmare. Of all the redevelopments in Cambridge, this place is by far the worst. It is hard to call it a scheme or plan since, apart from cb1, it is unplanned, an *ad hoc* disaster. One is hard pressed to read or hear a good word about it, other than in the propaganda of the developers. Until quite recently it was an area characterised by shabby neglect. Marshalling yards, sidings and warehouses fell into disuse as rail freight was superseded by road haulage. Then came piecemeal development of varying degrees of mediocrity, followed by the active vandalism of 'in your face' buildings which has aroused such strong feelings.

The earliest arrivals, from the 1980s, look positively dinky today – the little houses in Devonshire Road and William Smith Close, so small that four or five strides will take you in through the front door and out through the back. Around the same time came the first commercial buildings by the edge of the old cattle market, facing Cherry Hinton Road. It was a shame to see the open space begin to disappear, but these were not buildings of particular offensiveness. The Clifton Road industrial estate was no worse than one might expect, and it is conveniently out of sight.

*Bogus Victoriana at Ravensworth Gardens.*

Ravensworth Gardens (1999) was a more ominous sign of things to come; grandiose and expensive, though of slight construction, it indicated the pressure to pile people in. Its red brickwork is an odd choice in an area of old Cambridge yellow bricks, and the brick itself is bogus, being a skin or cladding over a timber frame. On ranges of buildings so large and tall, the 'Victorian' details look finicky and only serve to draw attention to the fakery of the design. Along Devonshire Road, their three storeys loom over the two-storey terrace opposite and shut out the light. Thus they fulfil all the criteria for modern speculative housing; superficial pseudo-Victorian references, dense concentration of residential units, and overbearing height and mass. More such overblown blocks have appeared further up the line at Cromwell Road and St Matthew's Gardens. One is reminded of Muthesius's flattering comment of just over a hundred years ago, when he wrote that England was the only advanced country where most of the people lived in houses, while continentals were 'imprisoned in giant multistoreyed barrack-like blocks'. What would he think of us now?

It was when the flats in Rustat Avenue were built on the former site of the Leica works, directly opposite the station platform, that the railway area developments first made a visible impact upon visitors to Cambridge. Their quality can be gauged by the innocent remark of an elderly visitor, 'What are those buildings over there? Are they factories?' Alas, no. People live in those bleak, white-topped warehouses with balconies like forgotten scaffolding, the perfect setting for a TV gangster shoot-out or a cops and robbers chase. Five blocks stand end-on to the railway, leaving views between to a jumble of lower houses. It is the sort of layout that probably looks passable on a plan but chaotic in elevation. Seen from the station platform, the three blocks to the left have rather more external merit than the two adjacent ones. They make no attempt to disguise their height with white paint; on the contrary, they emphasise it with a top storey in black. The angled slopes of the lift towers and penthouse top floors tilt in opposite directions and lend some interest to the roofline, unlike their unimaginative flat-topped neighbours. The coloured materials – red, buff and black – make for a striking effect, but one which is already a cliché. Scores of almost identical buildings can be seen alongside any railway line in and out of any city. Looking from the train window near King's Cross after an inadvertent slumber, you might wonder if you had actually left Cambridge station. For Rustat Avenue is London dumped down in Cambridge; an alien, a cuckoo in the nest. It is like finding travellers' caravans in a lay-by or tents on your lawn. It hardly says 'welcome to Cambridge'.

Exploring the complex, one encounters a wholly urban environment of hard materials; of bricks, paving and metal. At ground level it is difficult not to think of back-to-back houses, industrial buildings or even prisons. Metal

*The insultingly basic construction of warehouse-like units barely suited to human habitation gives visitors no hint of Cambridge's rich architectural heritage. Rustat Avenue, seen from Cambridge Railway Station.*

*The perplexing façade of Rustat Avenue's Bailey House - a shoe box with upmarket scaffolding tacked to its walls.*

grilles and gates are everywhere, metal balcony structures run from top to bottom like fire escapes, and one almost expects to see warders patrolling above. The ground-floor windows facing the railway are actually covered by spiked bars, and some are filled with naked breeze blocks, presumably inserted afterwards. There is some car parking under the flats, but that does not stop unsightly parking in the open, half on the pavement. There is nothing to look at except other flats, the railway power lines and cars. There is no comforting sense of enclosure, and the space between the blocks is a kind of no-man's-land. The lucky ones face Rustat Road and normal suburbia. It is a mercy that the old hawthorn hedge, boundary of a long-forgotten field, survives to screen these intruders. This development shows all the marks of the speculator – a collection of soulless boxes which no one in their right mind could take pride in.

*More bleeding edge 'design' at Rustat Avenue.*

*Facing page*

*Top: Battleship Belvedere, top deck bristling with guns, ever ready to repel the inadequately moneyed.*

*Bottom: The Levels, towering to six storeys.*

The real sign of horrors to come appeared in 2005 when the Belvedere went up. This, and the Cambridge Leisure Park opposite, radically changed the landscape here, and not for the better. It was Docklands intruded into an ancient university town. The scale is unfriendly, intimidating, inhuman. The worst aspect is the posturing of the tower. Allowing this to go up was a bad mistake, for it set a precedent which other developers have been swift to pursue, and the council will now have its work cut out to contain the stampede of property tycoons with pound signs in their eyes. Has any modern tower matched the distinction of the humblest parish church spire? Is the Belvedere helping to create a skyline the equal of Oxford or Venice? Of course not. Modern towers are ugly, pretentious and unneighbourly. Their flat tops, matchbox proportions and acres of glass simply don't fit in. They have without exception spoiled every ancient town where they have been let loose.

The sheer scale of the buildings also sounds the death knell of the 'rural backwater with a university', as Cambridge M.P. Robert Rhodes James once described the Cambridge of thirty years ago. He was not being complimentary; he was praising the development of the 1980s 'Cambridge Phenomenon'. But there is a lot to be said for backwaters in these days of incessant development, when the lifespan of commercial or public buildings seems to be little more than a couple of decades. So the cattle market is replaced by a tawdry piece of urban bleakness, and a few small shops by the sixth form college are cleared to make way for a giant warren built to house commuters on London salaries. It is an invasion, a takeover, an exploitation by outside interests. Gradual changes can be assimilated. Radical alterations, on the other hand, stir up alarm and resentment. People begin to feel they are strangers in their own town. Some might argue that towns do not 'belong' to anyone, yet it is human to want a sense of place, a home, a location with which one identifies. By length of residence, people come to feel a sense of ownership; it is their council, elected by local people, who should make the decisions that affect their locality, not outsiders with their own agenda. It is natural to resent bogus consultations and impositions from non-locals. The railway area exemplifies such impositions more than anywhere in Cambridge.

*Above: The dismal retro 'Futurism' of the Leisure Park's detailing - as shown by this lamp - cannot disguise its failure of design.*

*Below: The concrete wasteland that is Cambridge Leisure Park.*

The vile collection of buildings around the bridge is now visible from as far back as the Perse School, especially the frightful tower of The Marque (see Chapter 14). Coming nearer, the eye is also drawn by the cold blue of the Travelodge hotel, with its Advent calendar windows, and the Cambridge Leisure multistorey car park, a structure of almost unbelievable ghastliness – a pile of industrial fencing dumped down by the railway. A range of wholly undistinguished buildings faces the hotel across a waste of paving, cycle racks and four forlorn saplings. The whole of this corner is open and bewildering, with buildings at odd angles and the massive blocks of cb1 visible through the gaps. The attempt to create a comfortable, inviting piazza-style space is negated by the absence of firm enclosing boundaries.

To the left of the bridge stands the block called The Levels. The building thrusts forward as far as possible, further than the remaining row of Victorian shops, to make maximum use of the plot. One is suddenly plunged from suburbia into a London street. And The Levels are not so level; they rise towards Homerton Street to culminate in a six-storey corner tower. The building's name is an odd use of language, but one that is increasingly familiar as companies try to market their wares.

*The Leisure Park Travelodge - Cambridge's all-year-round Advent calendar.*

*Even for a car park, this pile of industrial fencing on Clifton Way is a shocker.*

*Homerton Street - chic sterility in stainless steel and stone.*

Looking down Homerton Street is to see a disaster area of barren urbanism. On the left of this uninviting precinct is the blank service side of The Levels. Natural greenery is almost entirely absent. There are some good trees at the bottom which will eventually soften the view – at least during the summer months – but for the rest it is tarmac, paving slabs, brick, concrete and metal, an environment hostile to nature. The pavement is lined with pointless steel bollards. Why must we have this clutter? Further on, the bollards turn into a veritable forest; are ram raiders a problem in this area? The signs on the restaurants are ugly, and there are predictable, numerous, depressing and officious warning signs outside Tripos Court, the gated community for students who in all probability will not be sitting the Tripos. There is no focus or cohesion to this pile of disparate buildings, and for all the references to the university it is a million miles in mood from Trinity Street or King's Parade. As in Rustat Avenue, 'gritty', depressing crime dramas could be shot here on the cheap.

Then we come to the Belvedere, a building whose name for once has a semblance of accurate description: a 'raised turret from which to view scenery'. At the top, and perhaps a floor or two down, there may be distant views of the river, the Backs and other green spaces, which may compensate

*From the street, the Belvedere's exclusive apartments look more like barred prison cells.*

*From the railway, the Belvedere might be a converted factory.*

for the immediate proximity of the railway track and other less agreeable prospects. But it is not quite the true belvedere, a modest structure looking out over a landscaped park. And whatever is said about 'landmark' buildings, the Belvedere is unlikely to feature on the tourist trail: the sight of it from the station will probably be enough. On a sunny afternoon in spring, it casts a cold shadow across the entire road.

Crossing the railway bridge is an unpleasant experience these days. In such a flat landscape one would expect something of a view. It is unsettling, therefore, to find buildings towering higher than the parapet. On one side, the Travelodge, with its drab brown façade and projecting blue panels, resembles forlorn council flats or tired 'social realismus' housing in the days of communist eastern Europe, while the multistorey car park could almost be a building gutted by fire. On the other side, the canyon effect is very evident where the railway line passes between the cliffs of the Belvedere and Tripos Court on the one hand, and the monstrous seven-storey flats of Kaleidoscope on the other. On the town side of the bridge, City House looks like a place where people are interrogated and tortured. In dark brick, with a forbidding, fortress-like appearance, it is the architecture of Mordor.

*City House - apparently modelled on a secret-police interrogation centre.*

*The junction of Hills Road, Brooklands Avenue and Brookgate, with its new expanse of tarmac and traffic lights.*

The aspect of the Brooklands Avenue junction is now altered by Brookgate, the newly built approach to the station. Any new road produces a deterioration of the environment as more space is given over to moving vehicles. And because people are anonymous, even invisible inside a car, the pedestrian or cyclist feels in an inhuman and hostile environment where a moment's inattention might mean death. The wonderfully tree-lined Brooklands Avenue and charming almshouses on the corner dwindle in significance under the baleful cloud of City House and the brick and tarmac of cb1.

A short way along Brooklands Avenue, a left turn into Clarendon Road leads to Kaleidoscope. The name sounds like fun, childhood, play, colour. Alas, the development that bears this name is not much fun at all. It is true that the buildings are coloured in places, and the shapes are built up as a child might play with wooden bricks. One might even call it infantile. Yet this is not a place for children. There is no grass and no play area, just hard surfaces and cars. This is a place for singles, childless couples, driven businessmen, London commuters. Billboards against the railway line tell passing train passengers, 'You could be home in just 10 minutes'. 'Home' ... a car park with flats, a denial of the real world of nature and green growing things. Barely any sun reaches ground level; four- to seven-storey blocks cast huge shadows. Block after block rises up amidst a sea of cars. The

**217**

spaces between buildings are cold and impersonal. No real enclosure exists anywhere. Residents can sit out on their boxy balconies and look at other balconies, or down at the cars, or they can cut their throats in despair. There is no useful public space in which neighbours might interact, nowhere to sit or stand or play or just watch the world go by. And space is at a premium in the blocks themselves; the above photo shows apartments packed to a density more suited to the massive conurbations of Tokyo, Mumbai and Mexico City than a medium-sized English provincial university town.

Kaleidoscope is advertised as 'the smart choice in Cambridge', 'a sophisticated lifestyle in a city centre location', statements that contain more than a touch of hyperbole. The city centre is a mile and a half away, and quite what is sophisticated about living in this soulless railway-side dormitory takes some finding. But anyone thinking of buying one of the 'stylish 2 bedroom apartments' needs to move quickly, lest they miss out and end up paying someone else's mortgage in rent; for these apartments are also 'the perfect investment'. It says much about the times we live in that an expensive box within earshot of railway station announcements, in a grassless environment, with nothing to look at but more boxes and cars, and with a sardine-can commute to London every day, is considered

*This and facing page: Colourful gimmickry cannot disguise Kaleidoscope's high density of occupation.*

sophisticated living. Or equally that the acquisition of one of these flats is seen as a means of making money out of the less fortunate. One-bedroom flats – what one might consider bog-standard accommodation for a solitary first-time buyer – were being marketed in November 2009 at 'from £54,000' for a 30% share, and in April 2013, two-bedroom flats were being offered at prices from £569,000. Like all the other densely packed sites that have been developed in recent years, Kaleidoscope is a human rabbit warren. It is hardly a place for living in; more like an overpriced hotel for the night. It is superficial, gimmicky, and ghastly.

Further along Brooklands Avenue lies 'Accordia' (2003-2011). If Kaleidoscope is meant to suggest fun and colour, Accordia is meant to suggest harmony and discriminating taste. You must be even more sophisticated than the Kaleidoscope dwellers to live in Accordia. You must be richer too; this development is award-winning and expensive. Indeed it boasts of being 'Cambridge's Premier Address' (although Cambridge Riverside claims to be 'the centre of excellence'). It is almost as hidden away as the government offices it replaced, and thus a good place to build fashionable apartments in

privileged seclusion. The Brooklands Avenue frontage is unobtrusive and partly screened – those wonderfully useful trees again. What one can see of the buildings from there is uninviting: flat-roofed boxes of no great distinction, though with a suggestion of decent proportions and high-quality materials, and indeed there are better things hidden inside Accordia, away from the rude gaze of the man in the street.

But – and so often there is a 'but' – the development shows little respect for neighbouring Hobson's Brook. One might forgive the developers for not thinking of this kind of detail, but did no council planner anticipate the outcome? The brook is a marvellous, miraculous survival. From what was originally the edge of open country at Long Road (until 'Great Kneighton' came along) one could follow its tree-fringed course all the way to the Botanic Garden. The illusion of rural tranquility was only faintly disturbed by glimpses of the low-density housing in Barrow Close and Newton Road, and the tennis courts and low buildings of the government offices that once occupied the Accordia site. Now, at the Brooklands Avenue end, Accordia has emphatically urbanised the setting. In winter especially, large rectangles of black-framed glass glare unpleasantly near through the trees. The area by the Cold War bunker is in particular need of screening; there is at present a horrid open view into the development, of cars, apartment blocks and all the things one does not want to see when walking by a quiet stream.

*For those of us not feeling the squeeze, Accordia, 'Cambridge's premier address', is the place to do some living.*

*Much is good about Accordia, especially its open green spaces and its simple designs, such as these on Richard Foster Road that recall to mind Jørn Utzon's Kingo houses.*

*Accordia's Glass Building - not what you want to see from Hobson's Brook.*

Finally, we return to the immediate vicinity of the station and to cb1, the 'Gateway to Cambridge'. The early plans for this showed much glass and glitter of a kind that seemed out of place, so much so that even the council took fright. Modifications were made (and continue to be made, seemingly in order to balance the books) and many of the buildings have already gone up. Until the whole scheme is complete it will not be possible to give a definitive assessment of its success, but that need not inhibit us from making observations on the progress so far.

The much heralded 'world class gateway' into the cb1 complex from Hills Road is an anticlimax: dull, boxy and inoffensive. It is a 'could be worse' entrance, and perhaps we should be grateful for that. The above photo, taken in May 2012, shows an uninviting prospect. Other buildings have since modified the view, and not for the better. Now, a dense grouping of gargantuan six-storey blocks suggests the grandiose schemes of Albert Speer in the Berlin of the Third Reich. Winding our way through them towards the station, we arrive at the one that faces the railway line (see photo on p. 195). Its façade is almost a hundred yards long, with little to break up the monotony. Why? Redevelopment of so large an area is a tricky test for architects; there is always the danger of mechanical repetition and paucity of ideas. It needs the skill of a Wren or a Hawksmoor, though not necessarily their classical style. Sadly there is no such skill here, not even with the placing of the bus shelters, which are open to the prevailing wind. And remarkably, this vast block of accommodation for Anglia Ruskin University students is right next to the luxury apartments in the converted mill.

*Brookgate - inexplicably named after the developer - is the banal new 'Gateway to Cambridge'.*

*Station Place. Is this the world-class entrance to Cambridge we were promised?*

The hoardings in Station Place are revealing; they display alluring pictures of King's College gate and Chapel, and the river by Clare, rather than showing the apartment blocks themselves. Such images – green space, a river and architectural masterpieces of the past – bear little resemblance to the reality of these railway-side buildings. It is typical of the modern age to reach out to grab a share of something – a landscape, an unspoilt country town, an unfrequented holiday resort – and in so doing to trample on it. Caravans cover Cornish cliff tops, camper vans toil up Hard Knott Pass, and meretricious mega-flats crowd in on provincial market towns, much of whose charm lay in their small size and populations, and the absence of inflated buildings.

*A hoarding in Station Place attempts to suggest excellence by association, mugging a world-class building to lend credibility to the developer's woeful architecture.*

We have yet to see what will finally be made of Station Road, the avenue that takes visitors towards the city. One inevitably fears a missed opportunity. The plans have been revised several times, as the scheme is so large and complex that any change in the economic climate has an effect on the viability of one or other aspect. The original developers, Ashwell, went into administration in December 2009, and the current company, Brookgate, has had further anxieties about funding. It has also had to contend with strong hostility to its designs. The council twice refused plans for enormous offices in Station Road, while local residents angrily opposed the demolition

of Wilton Terrace, an unassuming piece of Victoriana whose previously overlooked merits became obvious when contrasted with its intended replacement. But the developers have now got their way. The council, unable to risk the cost of losing an appeal, has capitulated, and eight- or nine-storey blocks will blight the avenue. The potential effect of this can be judged from the lower, but still massive, Microsoft Building, recently completed on the corner of Tenison Road.

Shortly before this book went to press, the latest plans for the station forecourt were published. It is difficult to tell from them exactly what the new buildings around it will look like, and how the scale of the area will change. Circulation of traffic is likely to be better (it could hardly be worse), but there is an awful lot of tarmac and little obvious protection from the elements. How different from the days before the station arches were filled in, and cabs drove behind them under shelter.

The route leading away from the station has already been damaged by the construction of Botanic House. It is not actually visible from the station forecourt, but only as one nears the end of Station Road. Yet that makes the shock of seeing it all the greater. It is not a bad building in itself – if you

*Above and bottom of facing page: the visitor's first impressions of Cambridge on stepping out of the railway station.*

*The monolithic Microsoft Building, viewed from Tenison Road.*

*Wilton Terrace, Station Road, awaiting demolition.*

like glass – and it does not look as if it will become shabby after just a few years. Its location and sheer size are the things that cause dismay. Its alignment to Station Road is perverse, giving no satisfactory focal point. It mimics the curve of the old buildings opposite, but they are turning the corner of two roads, while its own curve leads nowhere, and as a ground plan has no obvious logic in relation to the street. It is so large, so tightly fitted into the site, and so close to the trees of the Botanic Garden, that it looks to have been lowered into place by a giant crane. And, as pointed out in Chapter 10, the manner in which it overshadows the War Memorial is nothing short of shameful. Who are Pace Developments to tell us that we need this sort of 'dynamic environment'?

In the end, the cb1 scheme is not about improving a tatty area of Cambridge. The idea of making Foster's Mill the focal point of the 'quarter' shows hopeless poverty of imagination; the ghastly eyesore should have been pulled down. If anyone wanted to create a genuinely beautiful entrance to Cambridge they could do far better than this. There would be fewer and lower buildings for a start, and they would not all be cereal boxes. There would be green space, flowers, trees, and a real avenue down to the War Memorial. There would be a generous sheltered garden for railway users to wait outdoors in fine weather. There would be a new bus station, allowing

*Cluttered, chaotic, obstructed and ugly - the forecourt to Cambridge Station.*

Christ's Pieces to return to its original size. But the priority is profit, as it always is, and private profit at that. Any benefits to the community are incidental. What became of the library/museum/local heritage centre that was promised for Foster's Mill? Was it simply a way of justifying the retention of this eyesore until the plans for buildings of a similar height were accepted? It would seem it was never a priority; following the fire that destroyed much of the mill, no further mention was made of libraries, museums, cultural centres or the like. The area is 'prime development land' and so must be exploited to the last square millimetre. But must it? If we applied that principle to our private lives we would rent out our bedrooms by day and charge people to doss down in our cars at night.

And what has happened to civic pride? An area of considerable importance has been handed over to a developer to squeeze as much out of it as he can while making a few token gestures towards the concept of a 'gateway'. It is hardly the kind of ceremonial entrance imagined by Hawksmoor three hundred years ago. We live in a debased age, our priorities are awry, and the shocking mess of the railway area is the result.

**13**

# Things to come: Orchard Park

'Never construct for other people dwellings you are not prepared to live in yourself.'
[M.H. Baillie Scott]

Many English street names perversely refer to features of their locality that no longer exist, or which the building of the street itself has destroyed – Mill Road, Laundress Lane, Mercers Row, Abbey Walk, Ditton Fields. Others represent wishful thinking – Eden Street, Paradise Street, Antelope Way. The new development in north Cambridge, Orchard Park, seems to represent both types. The original orchards have long since gone and 'park' is an amazingly impudent description of a densely built-up urban estate. In fact this was not its original name; signs not yet removed proclaim it as Arbury Park, suggesting it was some time before the penny dropped with the developer's marketeers that this might not project the ideal image.

The view of Orchard Park from the Histon Road/A14 bridge is perhaps the most awful. This is a place older residents will remember as allotments, fields and orchards. Now it resembles the kind of ruthless exploitation one used to associate with the former Soviet Union. Indeed, on first seeing it, my mind went back to 1976 and a visit to Russia, where I saw apartments rising in the midst of half-cleared forest to the north of Moscow; it gave me the same sense of incongruity and brutal disregard for the landscape. This narrow belt of land would have been better planted up with trees. The inhabitants of Arbury would then have had a visual and aural barrier from the relentlessly lorry-laden A14, and the trees might have absorbed some of the traffic fumes. But apparently government targets have to be met, Cambridge must grow and more people must live here, even if it means building right up to the busiest highway in East Anglia.

When the A14 was built it was given a name to disguise its real purpose. It was called the 'Northern Bypass'. That sounded more reassuring than the 'Main Traffic Artery from the East Coast Ports to All Destinations Inland'. When bypasses were first thought of, the idea was to take them well clear of the places they were avoiding and to leave the land in between as a green buffer zone. Then commercial imperatives moved in, bringing garages, superstores and housing estates. The buffer zone became a kind of no-man's-land, 'ripe for development'. Why not 'ripe for planting woodland'? Well, there is less money in that. So the last remaining open space south of

*Welcome to...er... Orchard Park.*

the A14 is filling up with houses, right up to the very edge of the maelstrom of traffic. It has therefore proved necessary to build a wall as a screen and sound barrier. There is, of course, no hint of this in the marketing pitch. 'Trinity Gate at Orchard Park', advertised in HomesNow (23 June 2011), is shown alongside a photograph of the river by Clare and Trinity Hall, a picturesque scene geographically two miles distant and in spirit light years away from this A14 hinterland. One feels the Trade Descriptions Act needs to extend its scope.

The A14 apart, Orchard Park's other disadvantage is predictable. It is densely built, with too many three- or four-storey blocks and long terraces. Such a large and intensive development needs a skilful plan to minimise its impact, yet the impression given is of an unconvincing jumble of both layout and styles. Variety of style and material might work in a suburban estate where the buildings do not tower up conspicuously, but Orchard Park is highly urban. A layout of squares, terraces and crescents would bring a better sense of order to such density of housing, as witness the streets of Bloomsbury, Bath and Cheltenham. Instead, we have a hybrid plan, part sinuous and part grid-like, with few public areas or gardens. The residents, who have complained that so little green space is provided, have no sense of enclosure, and the scale of the estate is not concealed from them. A home should provide refuge from the world; there is little escape here from the ranks of staring windows and the feeling of being watched.

*Cell-like windows bring to mind a prison - the view of Ring Fort Road from the Histon Road A14 interchange.*

228

*The baffling architectural leitmotivs of Orchard Park - clashing colours, useless balconies and mannered rooflines.*

Future tree planting may improve matters, but no amount of concealment will detract from the height of the apartment blocks. The sense of claustrophobia is further intensified by the road plan; every apparently inviting side street or alley leads to a brick and concrete car-strewn wilderness, not the green haven one might have expected. In another perversity of layout, some of the houses face King's Hedges Road rather than being angled away from it. The early developments at Milton Keynes make an instructive contrast. There, trees screened the houses from busy roads, and two-storey buildings were carefully aligned to minimise the sense of being overlooked by neighbours, despite a high density of housing. Orchard Park has been unable to achieve this.

What of the styles within this warren? Some of the smaller units are attractive. These three-storey cubes, shown bottom left, have satisfying proportions and a restrained palette of yellow brick and white stucco. But their neatness and distinction only highlight the ugliness of much else — town houses disfigured by balconies resembling fire escapes, or apartment blocks unsuccessfully embellished with colour. In the photograph above, for example, there is an inharmonious clash of dark blue, pale blue and brick, giving the effect of something botched up – like a DIY car-wing repair. How long will it take for these colours to fade? In other rows there are slight variations of height to a degree that becomes irritating, fussy and confusing, especially when accompanied by a change of material. Yet where façades are not treated to embellishments, Princeton Gaol or Wormwood Scrubs come to mind. There are too many ill-assorted types of design and material for success.

*Rather better proportions and a restrained palette produce a more satisfactory result.*

One of the few focal points is the 'circus' framed by Chariot Way and Circus Drive. One approaches it along Chariot Way, but any expectation of arriving at an enclosed haven is wrecked by the road being driven straight through its centre. Why should a circular garden be bisected? Was this originally planned, or was it a later modification to accommodate traffic flow? Whatever the explanation for this oddity, it has several unpleasant consequences. There is a nasty view south towards the restless junction at King's Hedges Road with its cluster of winking traffic lights and flitting cars, while visible to the north is the ugly sound barrier against the A14, which spares one the sight of the motorway but not its noise. The road narrows to one lane at the centre of the circle to prevent cars rushing through, and therefore displays the obligatory signs and road markings to warn of this. Four 'decorative' bollards mark the place where one would have expected a fountain to be, or perhaps a circular sitting area. The green space is thus cut in two, and the dense screen of tree planting around it loses its enclosing value where the road breaks through.

*Above: The central garden of the 'circus' ruined by a road and its obligatory street furniture.*

*Left: Chariot Way, the southern range of the 'circus'.*

*Above: Lack of symmetry in the rooflines flanking the northern exit from the 'circus'.*

*Below: 'Fly-away' rooflines - a novel, frequently repeated and totally unconvincing feature.*

The buildings around this circus are equally perverse. Such a layout invites uniformity and symmetry, but only the southern segments provide the simple regularity of common features. The effect is marred somewhat by the corner 'towers', whose façades rise above the eaves of the roofline in a way that is unsettling to the composition. Rather than being integral parts of the whole, they give the impression of being stuck on. The two segments to the north, however, differ not only from the those to the south, but also from each other. The one to the northwest is the most successful design. Its end 'tower' is satisfyingly capped, the rooflines taking one's gaze down into the circus. Its neighbour to the northeast, by contrast, is confusing and restless, with jutting angles flying up in unresolved directions. Unlike a Regency circus, which was all about symmetrical restfulness, this circus has absolutely no repose, its logic being quite destroyed by this 3-D Futurist painting effect. Gaps between these curved ranges and their end 'towers' further diminish the sense of enclosure and allow a view of the cluttered angles of the buildings behind.

The traffic flow through the centre on a Saturday morning is almost continuous, and this is an estate that is not yet fully occupied. Even buses pass through. What should be a peaceful garden is thus harried by the seemingly inescapable motor car – as if the row from the A14 were not bad enough. The two benches on opposite sides of the perimeter actually face the wrong way; in the absence of any central feature they turn their backs to the open space and confront the buildings. It would be the same were you to sit on a beach with your deckchair facing the wall of the promenade. It is hard to see this space ever being used recreationally. To emphasise the dominance of the car, we find at the entrance to Chieftain Way twenty-one signposts or traffic-light posts, a dozen lamp posts and seven yellow bollards, while at the junction of King's Hedges Road, Arbury Road and Chariot Way there are over forty posts.

Walking north from the circus, the eye is caught by a 'stunt' building with a projecting roof like a wimple. Then on the left, the Premier Inn may be seen running parallel to the A14. This is well proportioned, and of a basic Modernist design that could almost have been put up in the 1930s – a horizontal range balanced by a vertical tower that correctly signifies the location of the entrance. Unfortunately it has fallen victim to the present fashion for coloured walls – of three different hues in this case – which succeeds in upsetting the overall harmony. The pale yellow is especially regrettable.

*Wimple Hall?*

*The Premier Inn exhibits clean Modernist lines and well balanced proportions.*

On nearby Ring Fort Road are some of the best buildings on this site. These apartment blocks are shapely and honest. Even so, there is a surface busyness created by the slatted sun filters and glazed balconies all-too-visibly filled with plants, tables, chairs and washing. But perhaps one is being too demanding. Maybe one should instead picture Naples and be glad.

*An example of Orchard Park's simpler, better-proportioned apartment blocks, on Ring Fort Road.*

Orchard Park is the product of the modern mentality that responds to pressures in the belief that they are unstoppable. Pressures to build more houses are accepted uncritically, and any piece of land caught between a city boundary and a new major road or bypass is automatically considered 'ripe for development'. It is a temptation to the developer, who can claim to be adding to the housing stock or 'bringing jobs', and who has his major access road already built for him. The idea of leaving the land open as a green barrier against the road, or of planting it up with trees, is never considered. But why shouldn't it be? What sort of city do we want? There is also the fatalistic acceptance that in the near future the population of our small island is doomed to grow to c. 70 million, and equally that Cambridge is a 'growth area' and must accommodate more people, more businesses and more buildings. These are regarded as 'market forces' and ineluctable. Yet what are 'market forces' but the agglomeration of individual decisions? It is not necessary to do what your neighbour is doing. Genuinely radical decisions that stand against the prevailing orthodoxy are perfectly possible and can be made to work. If that were not so, we would not have the National Trust, National Parks, the Green Belt, pedestrianised town centres and all other manifestations of decisions chosen in defiance of the existing 'conventional wisdom', decisions which have saved this country from the worst depredations of crass commercialism.

*Poundbury, Dorset: an alternative approach to creating new communities.*

*Stannon Street, Poundbury,
where a well-judged mix of
vernacular designs gives the
reassuring impression of a
long-established town.*

Cambridge has already made such decisions in the past with success, which is why until recently building heights were strictly controlled. Pedestrianisation was introduced despite complaints from shopkeepers that the city centre would become a ghost town if people could not drive right up to their doors. In fact pedestrianisation has made shopping a more enjoyable experience, and there is no shortage of people in town on a Saturday afternoon; indeed, the centre has never been more crowded.

An instructive example of standing against prevailing orthodoxies may be seen at Poundbury near Dorchester. Dorset had to meet its housing targets, particularly for low income families, and the Duchy of Cornwall was obliged to respond. Prince Charles therefore considered novel approaches to creating a new community. He had to endure a great deal of criticism, often silly and spiteful, on account of his imaginative and thoughtful views. To his credit he carried on regardless, and the results have been impressive. Critics of Poundbury have taken issue with the Prince's preference for vernacular and classical architecture. Given what this country has seen of Modernism this preference is hardly surprising. He is not hostile to good

modern architecture, as may be seen from his book 'A Vision of Britain' (1989), and he changed his mind about the British Library (which he had described as a dim collection of brick sheds) after seeing inside the completed building.

But his critics miss the point. Poundbury is not just about surface appearance or style. Most importantly, there was a plan which the community helped to create. A key element was to return to the idea of a 'walkable' town and to put people before cars. Before the motor car, the size of a settlement was generally limited by the distance people were willing to walk. Poundbury set out to be a place where no one was more than ten minutes' walk from most daily amenities such as schools, shops and places of work. There are no traffic markings painted on the roads, nor are there any traffic signs. Safety, for both cars and pedestrians, is built into the design. Structural 'events' – a tree, a fountain, a bench – are placed at regular intervals, and frequent changes are made to the shape of the roads, which periodically open into squares of different sizes. All this creates an element of surprise, which results in drivers going more slowly. How different from the dead straight suburban roads used as rat runs.

*Poundbury's historical references sometimes verge on the precious, but overall its use of English vernacular works well.*

The immediately striking thing about Poundbury is that it already looks like an established town. This is the result of careful planning, mixing vernacular and classical styles, and mixing different scales of building – just as is found in a town that has grown organically over many years. The attempt to replicate historic development is fraught with difficulties, and critics might well say that something potentially so anachronistic should not be attempted; that it can only end in pastiche. This may be a valid point, but looking at the results one is inclined to think that Poundbury, unlike Orchard Park, has succeeded. In particular, the rooflines and vistas have been more carefully considered at Poundbury, and the impact of traffic agreeably lessened. While one could possibly imagine a Modernist Poundbury that followed the fundamental principles of bottom-up planning, scale and layout, one might nonetheless doubt whether satisfactory results could be achieved without reference to traditional forms – pitched roofs and conventional fenestration in particular.

**237**

*Poundbury's 'affordable' homes benefit from the same attention to detail and high quality materials as are employed on grander buildings.*

Poundbury works because there has been real consultation to find out what residents want; at Orchard Park you take what you are given. At Poundbury, private and social housing alike has been built to the same standard using high-quality materials. Designs refer to traditional local styles and materials, avoiding prefabricated units and anonymous global uniformity. It has been planned not as a suburb of Dorchester but as an urban centre in its own right, with all necessary facilities a short walk away. The streets are quiet, intimate and full of visual interest. The scale is human. Above all, Poundbury has been designed for people, not cars. It has been a commercial success. It has a soul, say the residents. What do the residents of Orchard Park say?

**14**

# Things to come: faulty towers

For many years Cambridge fended off the ugly tower blocks that were so fashionable in the post-war period. They have catastrophic effects on open spaces and neighbouring buildings, spoiling their scale. They relate badly to the street and to old rooflines, and they rear their heads in unwelcome places, whether seen from near or far. In a city like Cambridge they are wholly unsuitable, and in consequence there has long been a deliberate policy to protect the skyline. In general, it was felt that nothing was to exceed the height of King's Chapel. The Holford Report of 1950 recommended a maximum height of 55 feet to preserve the character of central Cambridge, and Denys Lasdun's preposterous 200-foot tower on the New Museums Site, proposed in 1961, was rejected, though not without difficulty. Quite recently this sensible policy has been thrown aside and, following the unwise precedent of the Belvedere, the city is threatened with one 'landmark' building after another. Why is this?

Partly it is to find ways of accommodating 'growth' without encroaching too far into the Green Belt. Partly it is vanity. Some councillors appear to have become enamoured of 'landmark' buildings – deluded grand statements of metro glitz and aspiration. This is the sort of thing we expect to find in the City of London; it is the last thing we want in Cambridge. If you like metro glitz, go and live in the metropolis and stop commuting. The current height limit for a building appears to be ten storeys, but that in itself does not determine how tall it will turn out to be. Offices have higher ceilings than apartments: just look at the size of the windows in Botanic House.

In 2009, councillors started talks with architects and developers about tall buildings with a view to creating a 'Supplementary Planning Document'. Given the sensitivity of the topic, it is not surprising that public consultation and feedback were pushed well into the future. Since then, three 'landmarks' have already gone up, causing controversy. Early in 2010, knowledge of these talks leaked out, prompting Cambridge Past, Present and Future (formerly and more sensibly called the Cambridge Preservation Society) to hold a public meeting on March 3rd of that year to discuss the policy. Several dangerous ideas were floated. One was that there could be clusters of tall buildings away from the centre, as in Paris, with Marshall's airfield as a possible site. Another was that they might be placed at local centres in the suburbs, such as the Perne Road/Cherry Hinton Road corner where Budgens stands. Entrances to the city might be considered, including the station area. Or there might be tall buildings round the perimeter of green spaces such as Parker's Piece, emulating New York's Central Park. That any of these ideas could be seriously entertained is astonishing, yet some are already being put into practice. Two of Cambridge's most remarkable open spaces, the Botanic Garden and Parker's Piece, have been shamelessly spoilt by the construction of tower blocks.

*A surreal jump in scale on Hills Road - Botanic House rises behind its Victorian neighbours, each window almost half the size of their façades.*

At the southeast corner of Parker's Piece the old fire station has been demolished. It was a simple piece of 1960s architecture and whatever its visual shortcomings, it had the merit of being no taller than the rest of the low buildings around the green. The site has been developed by Grosvenor, who, so they said on the hoarding, have been 'creating great places in Cambridge for over 25 years'. So now we know who to thank. We are often told that there is a shortage of homes for ordinary people in Cambridge. Bugger that, say Grosvenor, let's have 99 'luxury apartments'. One might have thought that living by one of the busiest roads in Cambridge above a fire station would not be the height of luxury, but perhaps it is all right if you don't open the windows.

And there are plenty of them. The chief feature of this complex, called Parkside Place, is an eight-storey tower that affords 'commanding views over Parker's Piece'. It is just as much a disaster as Botanic House. The whole point about Parker's Piece is that it is a vast open space surrounded by trees. Until recently no buildings were substantially visible above the line of the tree tops, except for the atrocious Examinations Syndicate cube and the spire of the Catholic Church. A church spire is a pleasing and appropriate focal point. The last thing Parker's Piece needs is a pretentious Dan Dare tower just so that a handful of prosperous persons may have a fine view. What about everyone else's view – marred by this foolish erection just as Botanic House mars the view from the Botanic Garden? Such towers dislocate one's sense of scale and reduce the apparent size of open spaces. The windows are enormous compared to those of the existing terraces. The stone cladding is almost white and hopelessly at variance with the predominant grey brick of the area. Even the Brutalist concrete of the police station is grey and inoffensive beside Parkside Place, which displays all the arrogance of a Norman castle, clutching advantages to itself and sneering down at the peasants below. In what way, one might ask Grosvenor, is this 'landmark' nonsense 'a great place'? It is great only in size, and that is the

*Parkside Place rears its head well above the trees that line the south-eastern side of Parker's Piece.*

*Parkside Place under construction.*

real point, of course. In the guise of creating a 'landmark' building the developer can build higher, increasing the number of apartments and thereby his profits, at the expense of our townscape. Do any of the people behind this scheme actually live here?

Botanic House has already had frequent mention. It is difficult to imagine anything more inappropriate and insulting than this meretricious piece of boardroom vanity. Even the mature trees of the Botanic Garden are dwarfed by this seven-storey glass monster. It adopts a blatantly self-serving posture, awarding itself a fine view into the Garden while at the same time spoiling the experience of those inside. It intrudes heavily into every vista along Hills Road, while from Regent Street it forms an equally odious backdrop to the Catholic Church.

But the building's worst offence is that it literally overshadows the War Memorial. This was demonstrated on the first two Remembrance Day Services following its construction, on 13 November 2011 and 11 November 2012. Both days were sunny and the faces of those standing by Station Road were lit up, yet the soldier on his plinth stood in the huge shadow cast by the office block. There could be no more shameful indictment of priorities. A monument symbolising self-sacrifice, the highest form of service to the country, is dwarfed by a monument to self-service, greed and utter indifference to any value higher than that of making money. Depressingly, there is more of this crass glass and glitter to come on the adjacent site.

At the same time that Botanic House was going up, Cambridge University's Sainsbury Laboratory was being built inside the Botanic Garden. Displaying much more sensitivity to its location, this fine, low, well-proportioned and deceptively simple building, with its restfully subdued palette of colour and materials, deservedly won the 2012 Stirling Prize for architecture. Although a university laboratory, it has a public café, and presents a more open face to the outside world than does Botanic House with its depressingly predictable corporate arrogance.

In respect of its location, Botanic House ranked as one of the worst buildings to have been granted planning permission in Cambridge in recent years. That was until the construction of The Marque, begun in 2012. This ten-storey abomination on the junction of Hills Road and Cherry Hinton Road was first proposed several years ago as an eight-storey construction called 'Living Screens'. Early plans were rejected until the architect warned that it was this scheme or nothing: 'This is almost the last opportunity, the

*The quiet, restful and open Sainsbury Laboratory.*

*Plumbing new depths - Botanic House, with its smug and boastful advertising, makes a telling backdrop to the War Memorial.*

last chance to achieve something different on a site deserving of an inspired piece of architecture'. It seemed that the developers, after four attempts at getting it right, were never interested in getting it right at all, only in getting it through. However, it was another two years before they were given consent, in June 2010, though why is a bit of a mystery: the revised design was virtually indistinguishable from the earlier rejected versions, except for the fact that – incredibly – it now boasted an additional two storeys. Even more incredibly, councillors who had once condemned what they called a 'grotesque' design, which they feared would overwhelm the area, now decided it was 'bold and exciting', and praised it for its 'elegance' and 'beauty'. Said one, 'This is a highly talented and creative building' (sic).

It was a further two years before construction work began. Puzzlingly the site hoardings announced not 'Living Screens' but 'The Marque', a name of equal pretension for yet another 'exclusive' city development. The same hoardings proclaimed this Brobdingnagian structure to be 'Cambridge's Tallest Residence'. The developers evidently consider this an advantage, though others, who will have to look up at the thing rather than down from it, may beg to differ. It will be visible from Ely Cathedral tower, let alone many other nearer vantage points. At the current stage in its construction (summer 2013) it already dwarfs the ordinary houses in the immediate vicinity and exceeds even the height of the Belvedere Dalek, completing the utter ruination of the Hills Road bridge area.

The building steps up from three to four storeys before rising to a ten-storey tower on the corner. This is no slim, elegant focal point. It has the proportions of a double bed set up on end, its vast façade looking towards the Travelodge. The tower is not the only disastrous feature. Even the lower wings possess intimidating bulk, standing right up against the pavement and casting cold shadows across Cherry Hinton Road; along Hills Road they complete the canyon effect begun by The Levels and The Belvedere. So what is it that makes this building 'bold and exciting'? Surely not its shape, which is the familiar pile of cereal packets we have seen going up around the railway area. It is, we are told, the 'living screen'; a kind of heavy lattice of panels encasing the tower. In artist's impressions this might convince some. In actuality, the effect is likely to be less attractive. This dreadful collection of gormlessly gaping voids is banal in the extreme. Equally preposterous is the fact that the original version of this gimmick, which was key to gaining planning permission, proved to be unbuildable. As of August 2013 the

*The mid-morning sun shines through the skeleton of The Marque, giving an indication of the huge shadow it will cast when fully built.*

*A hoarding shows the finished article, a concrete bastion for the 'chic and sleek' rather than the man in the street.*

unclad building awaits a solution to a problem that should have been solved before ever planning approval was given. And this meretricious 'screen novelty' is hardly enough to justify the baleful effect of the development's overbearing scale. Astonishingly, the architect claimed to be creating 'an inspiring piece of architecture'. In fact it does no more than ape the worst excesses of the 1960s, as if, to adapt James Stirling's phrase, those responsible were deliberately setting out 'to fuck Cambridge'.

The officials who approved this outrage should feel disgraced, assuming they have consciences at all, and their names and faces should be prominently displayed on adjacent billboards so we know who to thank. How can such architectural vandalism be permitted, and in this city of all places? Were a sign needed that Cambridge is finished, and that decency in town planning is dead and buried, this fatuous building is that sign. The Belvedere was bad enough. Botanic House was worse. The Marque exceeds both of them in its sheer size, its social divisiveness, its pretentiousness, its harmful and inappropriate impact upon its surroundings, and its utter disregard for seemliness and architectural good manners, or anything other than private profit. Will this building enhance the landscape of Cambridge? Or render it more hideous? We already know the answer.

On the other side of the railway bridge, the developers of Kaleidoscope were intent on building a ten-storey tower, simply because others had been allowed to build towers. Their original, and contentious, scheme made no mention of this; now, a tower was deemed desirable in order to bring 'balance' to the development. A representative for the developers Crest Nicholson said, 'The context of this was trying to improve design, it wasn't about extra units' (Cambridge News and Crier, 10 March 2011). Councillor Margaret Wright begged to differ, and claimed that the proposals were intended to make the whole scheme more financially viable. It is hard not to agree. If it were simply a design issue, it would say little for the competence of those producing the original plan. But how many times have we seen developers get a foot in the door and then inflate their demands, like some unscrupulous door-to-door salesman who, if you are unwise enough to buy a duster, tries to sell you the entire contents of his case?

There are people, it must be admitted, who like living in apartment blocks, particularly if they have a good view. But that is not why we have them. Quite simply, apartment blocks bring a bigger return to developer and landlord, and help the council meet government housing targets. But is it a remotely enlightened policy to pack as many people as possible onto a site? As long ago as 1947, in his book 'London', the Danish architect Steen Eiler Rasmussen warned against flats: '...all the disadvantages of overcrowding are terribly increased in blocks of flats with many rooms under one roof, in large buildings with far too many inhabitants.' Privacy is reduced, noise is increased, well-being is depressed. A view of the railway track is a poor substitute for a view of one's own garden; luckless unfortunates lived like this in the old industrial towns, over a century ago. Progress has been retarded.

Furthermore, not all flats are as lavishly appointed as those at Accordia, off Brooklands Avenue. Those are flats for the wealthy. The ones by the railway give a better idea of the melancholy future for the young. House prices in Cambridge have soared to unreasonable heights in the past thirty years. The young buyer who then might have bought a two-bedroom terrace house in Romsey now struggles to afford a one-bedroom flat in a soulless block. Even humble Romsey has a sense of community and gardens. What community is there in a block of flats? No one should have to live like this, bereft of space, gardens, quiet and community. It was precisely this depressing anonymity that led to a reaction against the big city tower blocks of the 1960s, large numbers of which have since been demolished. In

*Just a few years ago it would have been inconceivable that Cambridge could be home to such buildings as these.*

*Top left: The Belvedere - the first invader opening the way for others.*

*Top right: Parkside Place - dangerously close to the historic centre, and exemplifying private privilege over public provision.*

*Bottom: Botanic House, big and boastful; a catastrophic intrusion on the very edge of the Botanic Garden.*

Cambridge, developers are clamouring to build them, disregarding the lessons learnt about the quality of life for high-rise residents and concentrating instead on the profits to be made from them.

Those who admire tall buildings are also in danger of forgetting two undesirable features. One is the wind. Winds whip round tower blocks with remarkable violence, up to four times stronger than on open ground. Pedestrians are buffeted, and the microclimate beneath a tall building is permanently colder. The other feature is shadow. Buildings like the Belvedere and Botanic House cast large, chilling shadows right across the road. On a sunny day, the difference in temperature between the open and the shady part of the street is startling and unpleasant. Both of these consequences were noted and deplored in other towns decades ago, yet still the towers go up. And there is a further point, apart from these two very palpable features: tall buildings are inhuman. They can only be properly seen, and maybe appreciated, from afar – standing beneath them one is normally aware only of the ground floor. If one does look up, details of people inside the building are largely lost above the fifth floor. The same is true for people inside the building looking down; they are more detached from the world outside the higher they go. They are insulated and isolated. Perhaps big buildings suit a certain type of person – Hitler, for example, was an enthusiast – but they are essentially anti-human.

There is a particularly frightful plan afoot for a nine-storey car park at Addenbrooke's Hospital. With space for 1,228 vehicles, it is to be 100 feet tall and clad in horizontal twisted metal ribbons of yellow, on the absurd assumption that this will 'refer' to the surrounding yellow rapeseed fields. Well, it might for six weeks a year – and not every year, if crop rotation is still thought to be a healthy practice. Given the remarkable height of the edifice, it might be better to paint it sky blue. A further three multistorey car parks of similar size are said to be needed within the next decade. No doubt this is thought to be 'sustainable'. Mightn't it be better to build three apartment blocks for the workers, to cut down on all this driving?

The recently completed tower of St Edmundsbury Cathedral in Bury St Edmunds is a proper example of a structure that enhances a skyline, and it shows what we can still do today if we are so minded. Tall buildings like this – a church, a temple, a mosque, a town hall – were once a focus and a symbol for the community. That focus is lost when too many buildings

*The Millennium Tower of St Edmundsbury Cathedral seen from Angel Hill.*

compete, as in New York, Hong Kong, Docklands; or if, as in Cambridge, they go up in random places with no thought as to how, or from where, they will be seen. And modern towers rarely posses the grace and elegance of those of the Middle Ages. Contrast the village with its church tower or spire, the building that once united the community and still draws the eye and composes the scene. Or consider the 18th-century prints of the Buck brothers, which show how much better towns were, visually, when there was a proper sense of hierarchy. The march of industry and technology has destroyed that in very many places and is starting to do so in Cambridge, where the wrong buildings are beginning to dominate. The towers that have gone up in the last few years – the Belvedere, Botanic House, Parkside Place and The Marque – are all private developments, usurping the visual pre-eminence of major public buildings. Some might say that the towers of Mammon are now the proper focus and symbols of our time. If so, let them do better than they have done so far to rival the beauty of the towers of past ages.

This book was virtually complete when the Cambridge City Local Plan was published. The plan does not rule out tall buildings, although it recognises the controversy caused by those that have recently gone up. As in much of it, there is the sound of stable doors being bolted to the distant echo of galloping horses. Equally disappointing is its tone of appeasement for fear of driving away the developers; a limit on building heights might 'stifle innovative and sustainable approaches to development'. This is feeble. What is innovative about a skyscraper? What is sustainable about a building that needs electricity for lifts and air-conditioning, and is exposed to winds on all sides? A policy limiting building heights would merely stifle tall buildings, and a good thing too. It is a pity the Belvedere was not stifled at birth; a building which, more than any other, opened the way to the despoiling of Cambridge.

# Conclusion: why we should care

The original purpose of this book was to poke fun at the unsightly side of Cambridge. But as writing progressed it became apparent not only that Cambridge was uglier than expected, but also that it was becoming much altered by rapid growth, and that many of the newest developments, far from improving the face of the city, were actively blighting it. Cambridge was being invaded by alien buildings, the earliest and most telling example of which was the Belvedere, whose construction began in 2005. As the plans for 'growth' began to gain momentum, it was clear that many more of these gargantuan horrors would soon be arriving. They did, and so fast that it was hard to keep up; within a matter of months, many details in this book had to be revised in order to take account of new developments.

Instead of writing about a few 1960s mistakes or Victorian disasters, I found myself increasingly dealing with the newest buildings. Some can be praised; too many cannot. Their chief qualities are brashness and inflated size. The comfortable, low-level, human scale of Cambridge is in danger of disappearing as residents are dwarfed by overbearing towers or herded into rabbit-warren flats. The designs are global, apparently taken from some pattern book, and they could be anywhere. Even plans drawn up by

*New developments dominate and over-whelm even in the heart of historic Cambridge, as here in Thompson's Lane.*

architects for specific sites show little respect for their locality; the 'bold statement', the 'sensation seeking stunt' is too tempting. Some councillors also seem intent on making the same mistakes as their predecessors did in the 1960s with their desire to show off their futuristic credentials. The architectural uniqueness of Cambridge in the world (matched only by Oxford) is being diluted by the copycat cosmopolitanism of apartment and office blocks, and especially by the threat of tall towers, the so-called 'landmark' buildings, which have the potential to ruin Cambridge utterly.

But it was not just the surface horrors that I found alarming; underlying causes and themes of equal, if not greater, concern became apparent the more I looked. These issues shifted the focus away from purely aesthetic matters towards the moral and social aspects of the built environment.

## Erosion of public space

One less obvious result of recent development has been the erosion of public space. Look at an old map of Cambridge and see what existed before Lion Yard and the Grafton Centre. There were streets, public thoroughfares. What has happened to them? At Lion Yard, St Tibbs Row, which formed part of a route between Downing Street and Petty Cury, no longer exists. Post Office Terrace and Alexandra Street are more or less replicated by the present passages through Lion Yard, but unlike the old streets they are no longer public rights of way at all hours. You may pass through from 7 am to 11.30 pm, and then the portcullises come down. These areas are monitored by CCTV and patrolled by security guards. Anyone attempting to take photographs there will be approached almost immediately by uniformed functionaries and given a hard time. Only the Big Brother posters and loudspeakers are lacking. What has happened here? What is this 'Walkways Agreement of 1998' which notices warn of? How do once-public streets become some firm's private property?

The same is true of the Grafton Centre; the thoroughfares of Gold Street and Eden Place have gone, and Wellington Street, Napier Street, Christ-church Street, James Street and Fitzroy Lane have all been truncated. This area too is now locked up at night. Public space has been privatised through deals between those who govern and those with access to large sums of money, just as it was when common land throughout the country was enclosed two centuries ago.

*Above: An intimidating list of regulations governs entry to Lion Yard, once a public thoroughfare and now private property.*

*Below: Lion Yard's east gate with portcullis lowered for the night.*

## Greater social divide

*Above and below: Harvey Road and Histon Road, where CCTV cameras and images of torch-wielding guards intimidate potential criminals and honest citizens alike.*

*Right: Posters in Station Place bus shelters trumpet luxury apartments beyond the means of most Cambridge residents, while all around lie retreats for the affluent and building sites promising more of the same.*

Equally unpleasant is the growth of 'gated communities', along with warning signs, security guards and CCTV. It is a sorry sign of our times. More people live alone, single-parent families are common, and apartment-dwelling exacerbates the social consequences. Flats are not as neighbourly as houses, and isolation seems to breed anxiety. Upmarket developments are promoted as 'luxury' and 'exclusive', displaying greater ostentation within secluded and secure retreats, while 'social housing' is in the main confined to areas not far removed from being ghettoes – often shoved up against the railway or a major road. In contrast to the enlightened philanthropic housing schemes of the Quaker and other nonconformist businessmen a century ago, we have 'that'll do' housing and pattern-book boxes. Meanwhile, anonymous inhabitants of exclusive apartments come and go, and retreat behind electric gates with coded keypads.

It also appears that far more luxury accommodation is being built than low-cost housing. Yet which group in our society is most in need of decent homes? The apartments that have sprung up in recent years are tailor-made for London commuters with London salaries. The local property news in January 2011 stated that 'Cambridge is now vying to become one of the top

10 commuter stations', as if this were remotely desirable. In March 2011 Cheffins ran a full-page advertisement in HomeoNow announcing their exhibition at the Move to the Country Show, 'which promotes regional property to London and international buyers'. Given the already over-crowded London trains and the lack of housing for people who work locally, is this the sort of thing we should be allowing?

## Erosion of local identity

Large developments of the kind we are now seeing also tend to diminish local identity. Nowhere seems to stay the same for long, landmarks disappear and new ones spring up almost daily. Lion Yard, and in particular its library, lasted only twenty five years before it 'had' to be changed. One wonders how necessary such change is; it is almost on a par with kitchen design, dated before you have put it in. The fact that so many new blocks of flats look identical to those in any other city increases the anonymity of our environment. And the names given to these developments often fail to have any connection with their locality. What are we to make of 'Accordia', 'Kaleidoscope' or 'Living Screens'? What is there to tell you where they are? Or even what they are? Accordia – a marriage guidance service? Kalei-doscope – a toy shop? Living Screens – a multiplex cinema? Locality, even honesty, is being usurped by inane lifestyle statements or euphemisms. Clay Farm had to become Great Kneighton; Arbury Park had to change to Orchard Park. Such renamings are risible; after all, if Trinity Hall, tired of being irreverently referred to as 'Tit Hall', rebranded itself as 'Living Scholars' we would naturally hoot with laughter.

Local opinion is clearly irrelevant to developers, as evidenced by a spokesman for Countryside Properties when commenting on the opposition to the name Great Kneighton; he said the company 'would never normally consult over a marketing name' (News and Crier 14 October 2010). Not a place name, then, nor a locality, but... a marketing name. We can only be grateful it doesn't have to have international appeal, like Cif (formerly Jif), though even that may not be long in coming, as we see from the headline in the News and Crier (3 November 2011): 'City property now popular with Far East'. And what gives the cb1 development the right to arrogate to itself, as a title, a postcode that properly belongs to much of southeast Cambridgeshire? It amounts to identity theft.

*Facing page, two contrasting faces of cb1*

*Top: the exclusive - but a postcode that extends almost to Haverhill is not as exclusive as they would have you believe.*

*Bottom: the inclusive - community artwork on Mill Road railway bridge welcomes visitors to Romsey.*

*The CB1 postcode area, devised in 1967.*

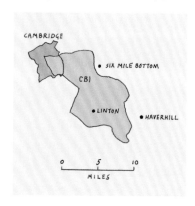

*Shoppers in chains. As in adjoining streets and malls, almost every trader here in Petty Cury is a national or multinational retail giant.*

Loss of local identity is not only an affliction suffered by housing. Familiar names disappear in foolish attempts at 'rebranding'. A notable example is The Garden House Hotel, whose name lives in history as the scene of the student riot of 1970. This has been preposterously renamed the 'Doubletree by Hilton'. That could be anything; even the word 'hotel' has been dropped. Where is the sense in that? It disregards the value and meaning of an original, authentic name for the sake of mere corporate 'visibility'. This is symptomatic of the growing influence of outside and alien voices.

## Globalisation

What is happening in Cambridge has happened elsewhere. The 'clone town' with identikit buildings and high street chain stores is not new, but until recently Cambridge had not suffered so badly. That has changed. The disappearance of small, local and useful shops was one of the first signs of decline, following the legislation of the 1980s which put pressure on landlords (especially charities such as the colleges) to maximise rental income. As Cambridge became a boom town during the emergence of the 'Cambridge Phenomenon', so rates and rents shot up to a level which made it impossible for otherwise viable businesses to survive. Thus we lost Joshua Taylor, Eaden Lilley, Bodgers, Taylors, Ropers, Grays the bookbinder and many others. Even bookshops could no longer cope, a startling state of affairs in a university town. Heffers, once running half a dozen shops, became a wraith of its former self, and this before the advent of Amazon. And when a firm as distinguished as Galloway and Porter closed, one knew the barbarians were inside the gates.

For the most part the old shops were replaced by chain stores selling designer goods, and while it seems there is not a street in the city centre without at least a handful of these cloned outlets, they seem to come and go with astonishing rapidity, their façades constantly changing. When shops appear to last no more than a year before closing, 'Next' seems the perfect generic name, possibly followed by an exclamation mark. Ironically, 'Next' is one of the chains that has persisted.

There is a curious paradox here, in that 'investors' and big retailers from outside Cambridge are eager to move in, while small local businesses struggle to survive. Hotel chains look to push their way in, yet at the same time hotels are sold when their corporate owners, with their fingers in many pies, become overstretched and have to 'rationalise' their 'portfolios'. In some respects, the appearance of Cambridge is now determined by people and events almost entirely unconnected with the city, except in so far as it is a place in which to invest.

## Property as investment

At one time a person might own or rent a shop, sell useful things and make a living. Now, a shop is a 'retail unit' and an 'investment opportunity' for a financial company that makes nothing, sells nothing and does no real productive work. Distant investment bodies are interested in only one thing, maximum return on their investment; collateral consequences are irrelevant to them. What is going on, for instance, when newly built offices remain empty for years, when pubs are sold by brewers for housing, or when the Christ's Lane development is sold for £33 million, only a year or two after its rebuilding? The sale of the Crowne Plaza hotel is instructive in this regard. It was recently put on the market for £35 million. Why sell it? Cambridge is allegedly short of hotel rooms, and a hotel ought therefore to be a useful and profitable business. The answer is that it is not an independent hotel, nor even just a hotel, but part of an 'investment portfolio' whose owners are in financial trouble. Crowne Plaza is technically owned by Shamrock Public Houses Limited, but this is a subsidiary of Quinn Property Holdings, which in turn is a subsidiary of Quinn Insurance Limited, an Irish company. QIL seemed to have overstretched itself to the point where it could not guarantee to meet its liabilities to policyholders. Consequently it went into administration, and it was the administrators,

*A far from isolated case: this popular Cherry Hinton pub has been scrapped by its brewery and offered up for sale in the expectation of quick profits.*

Grant Thornton, who made the decision to sell the hotel – one of QIL's 'non-general insurance business assets'. Thus the fate of the hotel was decided at least four removes from the people actually running it. And 'Crowne Plaza' itself is merely a brand name owned by InterContinental Hotels. Following the sale, the building is now styled the Cambridge City Hotel.

If we look at the Christ's Lane development we find a global dimension there too. The buyers are Henderson Global Investors, acting on behalf of its German joint venture, Warburg-Henderson. A spokesman for the firm said they were confident that 'the investment will outperform for our investors'. But what are they doing to 'earn' such profits? Charging retailers high rents. The News and Crier reported on 26 January 2012 that it was cheaper to rent retail space in London's Oxford Street than in the Grand Arcade, where some stores are paying up to £100,000 a year in rent, and into which many shops move only to find they cannot survive. Yet despite the expense, retailers are queuing up to get into Cambridge, which is consequently short of retail space. But is it? Not necessarily; it only lacks space for all the retailers who would like to come here. That is not the same as saying that we, the residents of Cambridge, don't have enough shops. This demand is an outside pressure, on a par with the building firms who would like to get their chance to profit from constructing all the housing we supposedly need.

*Speculative development at Botanic House. Plenty of room to spare after almost a year, contrary to the claim that Cambridge is 'desperately short' of office space.*

*The Homes and Communities Agency, briefed with providing affordable housing, inexplicably helping to fund the construction of exclusive luxury apartments.*

In these developments we see outside financiers determining outcomes, and councillors powerless against big money, or in some cases actively welcoming it. Monstrosities like Botanic House and The Marque are the result. Sites are developed by distant corporations with the intention of squeezing out every last penny of profit, irrespective of almost any other consideration. Shops come and go, unable to make a living even in a boom town, thanks to exorbitant rents and rates. Commercial buildings are frequently speculative, and not designed with specific reference to the people who will actually use them. Buildings are put up when they are not needed, as an investment in anticipation of a future profit, and housing goes up of a density, type and location that no one in his right mind would choose; for all the advertising blurbs about 'choice' you simply have to take what you are given. You might have fancied that detached house in the suburbs with its spacious garden. Bad luck; a developer can pay more than you can because he is going to fill the garden with flats. And as long as he can do enough to secure planning permission, the impact on the character of the neighbourhood does not concern him. After all, he doesn't have to live there. It is difficult to see any real accountability in all this. Cambridge is, in effect, becoming a commodity to be bought or sold for profit, a 'resource' to be 'maximised' for the benefit of people who do not live here; and it is being disgracefully disfigured in the process.

## Pressure to grow

The problems considered so far – globalisation, the erosion of local identity and community, the property gold rush and the increasingly marked social divide – have left ugly footprints in other towns. But Cambridge faces an even bigger threat to its character from the pressure to grow and the government's recent proposal to relax planning controls in favour of development. At the same time, the voice of the local resident is unwelcome and ignored. In June 2011, city councillors voted against holding a referendum on the scale and speed of Cambridge's growth. There is only one reason why referenda are refused; the authorities fear the 'wrong' result. Almost every week the local paper shows abundant evidence of opposition to current trends.

*A rabbit punch to the Green Belt - urban Cambridge now stretches for three miles to the southwest. Contrary to what the cute billboard implies, the Trumpington Meadows estate will obliterate the real meadows, along with their wild flowers and wildlife.*

In any debate – if any is allowed outside council chambers – the following questions should certainly be considered. What is the optimum size for a place that is agreeable to live in? What is the tipping point in population and area beyond which the amenity of Cambridge is destroyed? When does a pleasant town become a metropolis? Do we want to become another Birmingham? Who wants Cambridge to grow, and why? Is it the Government, their quangos, developers or local people? What authority does any person or group have to decide this? Do those who live here have a superior right over those who don't? What accountability is there?

*Facing page*

*The first phase of the NIAB site development along Lawrence Weaver Road. The size of the junction with Huntingdon Road reflects the volume of traffic that will be generated by 1,780 new homes.*

Some want to see Cambridge literally double in size – 250,000 is seen as the threshold beyond which 'rapid transport' systems are viable. Expansion would also extend the area possessing the cachet 'Cambridge', something that businesses are keen on. The name 'Power Jet Sewage Solutions' apparently carries more kudos when prefixed by 'Cambridge', which implies a relationship with academia. But in fact companies based as far away as Peterborough could still call themselves 'Cambridge Research Associates (Peterborough)'. Cambridge does not need to double in size to achieve this.

Promoters of growth like to talk about the jobs and wealth it will bring; they are less keen to talk about the attendant problems, which are huge. Rapid expansion puts pressure on the area's infrastructure, but the consequences are often brushed aside in the rush to profit. In August 2011, for example, councillors and the Highways Agency dropped their opposition to the building of 1,780 homes on the former NIAB site in Huntingdon Road, even though the previously required upgrade to the A14 had not taken place. And ensuring good-quality building design that properly meets residents' needs in such developments requires genuine consultation, not the hasty construction of off-the-peg designs. Provision of water and the disposal of sewage are still treated as somehow minor problems, something for water companies to solve. As for the problem of traffic congestion, it is probably insoluble while so many are wedded to cars and commuting. Go to Birmingham and take a good look before demanding that Cambridge should expand.

But the pressure to grow seems to be fatalistically accepted everywhere. Even the Cambridge Preservation Society has pusillanimously rebranded itself as 'Cambridge Past, Present and Future', which could just as well be the name of a development quango. At the seminar on tall buildings in March 2010, its chairman said, 'Cambridge must continue to grow if it is to maintain its economic and social prosperity'. That might have been the head of a building firm speaking. The 'core problem' was how to 'manage growth' and reconcile it with maintaining the special character of Cambridge. The city council said much the same in its publication 'Cambridge Matters', Autumn 2011. An article entitled 'Managing the growth of Cambridge' stated: 'The city council is updating the current local plan to cover growth of the city until 2031. The aim of the plan is to enhance Cambridge as a great place to live, work and study while maintaining the historical buildings and natural environment'.

*'Maintaining the natural environment' at Long Road. The main access road to Great Kneighton under construction.*

These sentiments have been expressed many times in the past. In 2004, the East of England Plan stated: 'New development is often seen as a threat to the quality of life and attractiveness of an area...' and added that local identity should not be compromised by 'anonymous and insensitive new development' (paragraphs 4.81 and 4.82). In the introduction to

*Worts Causeway, looking towards Netherhall Farm and the city's edge, which is creeping ever closer.*

'Cambridge Townscape: an analysis', published by the city's Department of Architecture and Planning in 1971, we read that it is 'important to ensure that those qualities which create the essential character of the city are not compromised'. The introduction to the Holford Report (1950) pointed out that Cambridge was perhaps the only true university town in England, implying that Oxford had been ruined by the Cowley motor works. 'The question is whether it can control its own destiny in the face of a multitude of unplanned events that will certainly tend to change it. When these changes come, and even before they take place, can they be arranged to maintain and enhance the essential character and virtues of the town?'

Predictably, these statements of intent have not been entirely effective. The 'robust green belt boundaries', which in 2004 it was hoped would persist until 2021, were weakened almost before the ink of the report was dry on the page. The government's recently published National Planning Policy Framework (March 2012) contains a 'presumption in favour of sustainable development', to which the city council must adhere. Already some 'events' are no longer unplanned but deliberately sought by local planners. Development is seen as synonymous with growth, and the assumption of the desirability of growth, i.e. the spread of buildings, is not challenged. Yet it is equally a development to return industrial land to the wild, as at the old quarries in Cherry Hinton, now a Site of Special Scientific Interest. As for the spread of 'anonymous and insensitive new development' – just look around. The struggle for civilisation against the barbarians is never ending.

The trouble with all of this is that people want to have their cake and eat it. Yet the whole notion of 'sustainable' growth is unrealistic. Cambridge cannot be both a vast high tech metropolis and a pleasant small town in which to live. Either you have more growth, more people, more traffic, more buildings, more noise, more crowded streets, or you don't. You cannot grow and yet stay the same. You cannot tarmac your front garden for car parking and at the same time keep your lawn. Furthermore, attempts to weigh the costs of development against the benefits, as in the new Local Plan, are misleading. Such costs (or losses) are not felt temporarily, as when you write out a cheque and think no more of it once you have handed it over. The costs of development are more permanent, seen and felt in the environment by everyone every single day. The benefits, by contrast, are more selectively bestowed.

**263**

## Planning controls

If growth is unstoppable, we will have to get used to the idea that the Cambridge we know will cease to exist. There will not be gradual change of a kind that can be comfortably assimilated. Cambridge will change rapidly, to a far greater extent than at almost any time in its history, and the greater the haste, the greater the likelihood of ill-considered blunders – look again at the area by Hills Road bridge. Current planning controls can do little to restrain developers and their desire to 'make a fast buck'. Yet at just the time when we therefore need more effective controls, the Government wants to relax them in favour of 'fast track' development. The Town and Country Planning Act (1947) is being revised to create a presumption in favour of 'sustainable development' and to remove the clause that gave recognition to the value of 'ordinary countryside'. A refusal of planning permission will now be pointless, since a developer's appeal to the Inspector is almost guaranteed to be upheld.

A corollary of this is the growing arrogance of developers. While they pretend to be philanthropically meeting the 'desperate' housing shortage, they are quick to turn nasty if their inflated, profit-maximising plans are rejected. In February 2012, proposals by Weston Homes for 124 properties in Cromwell Road were rejected following local residents' criticisms that they were a 'recipe for buy-to-let'. Almost all of the properties would have been one- or two-bedroom flats, creating a dormitory of transient occupants rather than a proper community.

In May the developers brazenly submitted a new and even larger scheme of 136 homes, threatening to take the matter to appeal if this were rejected. A spokesman for the residents said, 'Weston Homes seem to have completely ignored the planning committee's concerns about this development being unbalanced and a recipe for buy-to-let and short-term occupancy'. The chief executive of Weston Homes said:

'I do not see how such a short-term view [by the Council], which may appease a small number of very vocal Nimbys, would assist the vast majority of ordinary hard-working people in Cambridge struggling to get a foot on the property ladder ... sadly it does appear that the final decision on the scheme will ultimately be taken out of Cambridge City Council's hands.'

*Delusional hoardings in Cromwell Road illustrate apartments which are actually built next to railway sidings, at a distance of a mile and a half from the Backs.*

This mixture of twisted logic, condescension, name calling and threats destroys any credibility the developer may have had in claiming to bring benefit to the community. 'Gimme, or else!'

The speed of change in Cambridge is already so rapid as to seem out of control. Developers are moving in like jackals. They scent the weakness of the council – not necessarily its will but its actual powers – to restrain unbridled greed. In some instances the planners themselves, alas, welcome 'cutting edge' developments, and such is their taste that it seems to lead largely to horrors like Botanic House, Parkside Place and The Marque. In other cases developers promise community facilities, not from philanthropy but in order to secure planning permission that might otherwise be refused. If their proposals are still unwelcome, they can go to appeal. They can put in schemes far grander than they intend, then resubmit the lesser scheme they really wanted in the guise of having met objections of over-development. Having got permission, they can then modify or add to the scheme with relative impunity. How many inappropriate schemes can the council hope to fend off? How many appeals can they afford to challenge?

If anything, we need tighter controls. Cambridge, like other places in the South East, is increasingly at the mercy of market forces, outside pressures and big schemes encouraged by quangos and central government. 'Strategic planning' has its uses, but it seems to encourage megalomania and an arrogance that dismisses local concerns and fears: chuck in the word 'eco' or 'sustainable' and you think you have done enough to pacify those tiresome small-minded locals. If they become too vociferous you can throw the word 'Nimby' at them. These are not arguments; they are slogans and taunts, resorted to by those who have failed to make their case rationally and convincingly. In fact, most people are Nimbys, and rightly so. It is an attitude based on experience – post-judice, not prejudice. We know that the developer has his own agenda and it is not necessarily ours. Controls should ensure that any development clearly demonstrates its benefits and architectural merits to the existing community. And if they do not pass muster, there should be no possibility of railroading proposals through. On a smaller scale, the Bournville Village Trust showed that it is possible to insist on high standards and prevent unsuitable, ugly developments. In consequence it is one of the few places in Birmingham where anyone might actively choose to live. Where there is a will there is a way.

## Quality of design

After millennia of 'progress' it seems reasonable to expect quality of design in even the humblest object, to hope that cheap need not mean nasty, and to assume that lessons have been learned. When it comes to building, there is even more reason to expect the elimination of cheapskate mediocrity. Building affects everyone, and it matters very much that we should have a seemly and humane framework for our lives. No one should have to live in a dump or in fear that a speculative developer is about to turn the neighbourhood into one. It is therefore all the more outrageous that in so short a time Cambridge has been blighted by so much poor design, especially in the area by the railway.

One would think that quality of construction could these days be taken for granted, and that buildings will keep out the rain, doors will not jam, bits will not fall off and so on. Remarkably this is not always so. A new house in Cambourne proved to be so badly insulated that the heat escaping from the roof was detected by a police helicopter using thermal imaging, and the luckless householder was visited on suspicion of growing cannabis in the loft. There is also a greater use of render and timber cladding which does not weather well and soon looks shabby. This is presumably a convenient economy for the developer but not necessarily for the householder in years to come.

Quality of design in respect of style, of outward appearance, while to some extent a matter of taste, does seem to be wanting in new buildings. Why are so many new developments instantly derided? Is it because the ordinary man has no aesthetic judgement and fears anything new? Surely not. A really good building is unlikely to be controversial: its quality will be immediately apparent. Older readers may remember the photograph in a sherry advert some thirty years ago which showed an immaculately dressed horsewoman and her mount crossing a field: 'One instinctively knows when something is right', ran the caption. It was a neat use of a truism, and its converse is true. I have yet to hear anyone condemn the Jerwood Library and I have yet to hear anyone praise cb1. And where is the quality of design in the flats on Rustat Avenue? What does our instinct tell us about these boxes, which one person took to be warehouses with fire escapes attached? One could almost picture people on pallets being wheeled in and out of these basic human storage units. Again and again in housing we see skimped and pinched proportions, poor pastiche, inadequate landscaping, overcrowding and dismal outlooks. In offices we see unsympathetic materials, glare and glitter, inevitably built to an overblown, domineering scale.

*Banham's Close, where expensive riverside homes come ready fitted with tacky-looking loft conversions.*

We should be trying to create the listed buildings of the future. In a city as full of historical resonances as Cambridge, we should be building with reference to, and respect for, the best of the past. There is no such thing as a clean sheet, unless everything of yesterday is destroyed. That was the big mistake of the 1960s and indeed of earlier Modernism, trying to break entirely with tradition. The results were frequently lamentable. There have been modern buildings of genuine originality and quality, though the best will often be found to have roots in one or other earlier tradition. A more common result, however, is simply a version of the currently fashionable. Thus, in the buildings constructed in the past five to ten years, we have seen the same gimmicks appear – the 'Juliet' balconies, the skis jutting from the rooftops, the feebly disguised top storeys of tall blocks, the wooden cladding, the 'vibrant' coloured panels or stucco, and the not-quite-flat, slightly tilted roofs. The best designs are those which do not try to be clever, but which show good manners towards their neighbours and the neighbourhood. A straightforward use of a few materials produces quieter, more harmonious buildings than does the use of a confusion of colours and finishes in an attempt at variety. In general we do not need buildings to shout at us. Furthermore, we need buildings of such quality of material and design that they will last, that people will be proud to live or work in, and that will not need to be wastefully pulled down in less than half a lifetime.

*A grouping of three homes in Cavendish Avenue (2010), an example of modern design rooted in tradition, and proof that looking to the past for inspiration does not have to result in mere pastiche.*

The quality of design might be improved if the press gave more space to critical discussion of buildings. Films, television, theatre and popular music are all regularly reviewed, why not architecture? There is enough building going on to warrant it, and buildings have quite as much impact as these other arts, and arguably a more lasting one. And where it is within the council's power, perhaps there could be public competitions for building developments and more scope for public comment. How were the architects chosen for Lion Yard or cb1? It is true that there have been exhibitions of proposals, and the local paper is good at reporting on planning matters, but at the same time ugly buildings and crowded developments still get through, suggesting that local objections carry little weight. There is room for greater public information, education and debate about contemporary architecture. It would benefit both the public and the architect or developer if designs were explained, for it would tend to eliminate ill-informed criticism and also encourage developers to be more responsive to public reactions.

## Listed towns

We have listed buildings, listed trees. Why not listed towns? It is not just the beauty of individual buildings that make a town attractive; it is the collection of buildings, their setting in the landscape, and their overall size that achieve this. Some towns are so important architecturally that it would be vandalism to change them beyond recognition. That does not mean no change, but it does mean deciding that some towns are at their optimum size and should grow no further, that their ambience and function should suffer no major change. There is the possible danger of stultification, but without controls fine places are ruined or spoilt, potentially for ever. Bath, for example, was disfigured in the 1960s by tower blocks which are still there today. And merely preserving an ancient centre is not enough if development continues unchecked around it. How long would Cambridge last as a modest-sized town, if ringed with 'eco-villages'? How long before there would be pressure to fill in the gaps? Welcome to Megalopolis.

## Finally

Cambridge needs moderation in its buildings. It needs buildings that fit in, not ones that show off. It needs to avoid ruthless, ill-judged statements of 'superiority' and glassy tower blocks that will blight the city for generations. It needs tighter controls and greater emphasis on quality and durability, not on cost-cutting and private profit. It needs better local public participation to help create a city one can take pride in, and it needs to curb the influence of outside interests to prevent profit from being the sole consideration. And why not have a competition to identify the eyesores that need to be demolished?

Put the onus on the developers to do a good job in return for their profits, give them firm boundaries and don't let them exceed them. No more resubmissions and appeals which scale down from a ludicrous over-development to what the developer really hoped to get away with. No more 'application creep' – the extending of plans once the first permission has been granted. If the first plan exceeds the brief, there should be one more chance to get it right and no appeals. Do it once, and do it well. Whose town is it anyway?

One is drawn back to the observations made by William Holford in 1950:

'One cannot make a good expanding plan for Cambridge. If, however, the citizens of Cambridge decide that they are out for quality – to make the best possible town of 100,000 or even 125,000, and then stop – then we think there is every hope of making Cambridge something very fine, not only in the centre but in its suburbs, in East Road and along its approaches.'

Some sixty years later it seems necessary to reassert this view. Much damage has already been done, and in a very short time. But if the present rate and type of development is allowed to continue, it is difficult to see how we will be able to hand Cambridge on to future generations unimpaired, let alone improved.

Cambridge has meant something special for centuries. With its university and colleges, it stands for civilisation almost more than any other place. Its unique buildings and open setting embody that spirit. But Cambridge has become a city of cranes. The buildings that now begin to dominate represent a very different spirit, aggressive and ugly. It is profoundly depressing. Will this unique place, after being exceptionally preserved for so long, fall victim to acts of greed, folly and vandalism? Is the face of civilisation to be mutilated by barbarians? If so, posterity will have much to condemn.

# Index

Page numbers in **bold** denote illustrations.

*'Similar properties required.'*